MUSIC THEORY

Special Topics

MUSIC THEORY
Special Topics

EDITED BY

Richmond Browne

School of Music
University of Michigan
Ann Arbor, Michigan

ACADEMIC PRESS
A Subsidiary of Harcourt Brace Jovanovich, Publishers
New York   London   Toronto   Sydney   San Francisco

ACADEMIC PRESS, INC.
111 Fifth Avenue, New York, New York 10003

United Kingdom Edition published by
ACADEMIC PRESS, INC. (LONDON) LTD.
24/28 Oval Road, London NW1 7DX

Library of Congress Cataloging in Publication Data
Main entry under title:

Music theory, special topics.

Includes bibliographical references and index.
Contents: Pitch-class counterpoint in tonal music /
William E. Benjamin -- Poetic and musical rhythm, one more
time / Barney Childs -- ET Setera: some temperamental
speculations / Carlton Gamer -- [etc.]
1. Music--Theory. I. Browne, Richmond.
MT6.M9621   781   80-70592
ISBN 0-12-138080-7   AACR2

PRINTED IN THE UNITED STATES OF AMERICA

81 82 83 84   9 8 7 6 5 4 3 2 1

To the memory of
THOMAS CLIFTON
1935–1978

CONTENTS

4

MUSIC AS METALANGUAGE: RAMEAU'S FUNDAMENTAL BASS

Allan R. Keiler

5

SOME INVESTIGATIONS INTO FOREGROUND RHYTHMIC AND METRIC PATTERNING

David Lewin

6

PROLONGATIONS AND PROGRESSIONS AS MUSICAL SYNTAX

Charles J. Smith

LIST OF
CONTRIBUTORS

William E. Benjamin, Department of Music, The University of British Columbia, Vancouver, British Columbia, Canada V6T 1W5

Barney Childs, School of Music, University of Redlands, Redlands, California 92373

Carlton Gamer, Department of Music, The Colorado College, Colorado Springs, Colorado 80903

Allan R. Keiler, Department of Music, Brandeis University, Waltham, Massachusetts 02154

David Lewin, Department of Music, Yale University, New Haven, Connecticut 06520

Charles J. Smith, Department of Music, The University of Connecticut, Storrs, Connecticut 06268

PREFACE

In its present professional mode in the United States, music theory is characterized by diversity of topic and range of investigative method. *Music Theory: Special Topics* presents the imaginative and carefully argued views of six prominent theorists, each addressing an important theoretical issue of his own choosing. The volume is quite fairly representative of the intellectual liveliness of the field.

The various articles intersect across the most important traditional areas of concern. Tonal music, for instance, has long posed a problem, which might be stated as

1. the definition of the special relation between pitches.

A more general problem involving pitches and other phenomena involves

2. the definition of special relations in time.

A yet more general problem, transcending music, but not lacking in interest to theorists, could be stated as

3. the definition of relation, and of proper systems.

And, of course, the really general problem is always

4. the definition of definitions.

The distinguishing feature of modern music theory is its concern for the hierarchy I have briefly described. Each of the articles in the present volume displays an awareness of the cross-sectional nature of music theory.

Thus Keiler, in examining Rameau's figured basses, concludes that they are musical versions of analytic statements. His work draws heavily on modern linguistic technique and is critical not of Rameau's insights, but of the systems available to him.

Benjamin, using modern language, sees the underlying connections of harmonic progression as pitch-class lines. He can therefore discuss Schenkerian notions of counterpoint by sophisticated use of hierarchical distinctions unavailable either to Rameau or to Schenker.

Smith sets forth the idea of comparative analytic strategies using quite novel criteria: appropriateness and interest. He rightly calls attention to the traditional sense of a piece as a strategy for setting forth musical ideas, but insists that the hearer brings an arsenal of possible relations and systems to the encounter.

Theory is coherent explanation and rationalization when applied to objects created by persons of free will. It is not merely hypothetical, nor is it necessarily scientifically predictive. Thus, in its most productive mode theory is critical and speculative. Childs, in a major effort by a distinguished student of American music, sets forth in this volume a thorough review of temporal innovations in the music of the last 30 years, in the context of an equally thorough criticism of received rhythmic terminology.

Gamer carries the systemization of equal-tempered systems to the extent of suggesting processes for composing in other than twelve-note worlds, generating along the way the idea of syntactic models derived by extrapolation from systemic details.

And Lewin, in setting out a numerical model for assigning accent in metric interpretations of small-scale abstract rhythmic patterns, seems to sum up the role of theorist which pervades my description: the theorist as analyst, language-critic, system-maker, and predictor of possibilities in music. It is hoped that the publication and dissemination of articles as stimulating as these will embolden theorists and musicians to the continuing task of exploring and explaining music.

The editor thanks the authors for their gift of time and intellectual capital in this venture, and wishes also to thank the staff of Academic Press for its efficient support of *Music Theory: Special Topics.*

1

William E. Benjamin

PITCH-CLASS COUNTERPOINT IN TONAL MUSIC

Harmony as a discipline would appear to have had its day. As the author of a popular textbook puts it, "the term *harmony* is virtually useless. Supposedly, harmony deals with the study of chords, counterpoint with lines. But such a statement overlooks the basic fact that lines flow together to make chords, and that the only reason that chords follow in a certain order is that the lines lead them there. If harmony books make any sense, it is because they deal with musical motion—that is, counterpoint."[1] It is symptomatic of where we are that this author, while seeming to state the obvious, can slip by us a highly debatable proposition—that tonal chord progression is wholly a function of the linear structure of tonal music—and, in so doing, imply the futility of over 200 years of work in harmonic theory, work which attempts to expose the extracontrapuntal aspects of music in the tonal period. Where we are, of course, is in the time of the Great Post-Schenkerian Orthodoxy, in which it has been possible to write a treatise on tonal theory the table of contents of which makes no mention of "harmony," "chord progression," or "subdominant triad."[2]

My concern here is precisely with matters about which there is supposedly nothing more to say, that is, with the theory of harmony, or, as I prefer to think of it, the theory of pitch-class counterpoint. The concept of harmony I have in mind is, I believe, of potentially wide application, since it is at the level of pitch-class structure that the remarkable diachronic stability of the tonal system is most in evidence: Consider, for example, the

1. Leo Kraft, *Gradus: An Integrated Approach to Harmony, Counterpoint, and Analysis,* Book I (New York: Norton, 1976), p. 30.
2. Peter Westergaard, *An Introduction to Tonal Theory* (New York: Norton, 1975).

1

MUSIC THEORY: SPECIAL TOPICS

durability of the technique of circular motion via the diatonic circle of fifths.[3] In all its particulars, however, the model I will propose will apply more convincingly to some tonal pieces and less so to others. I am not bothered by this because in presenting a model of harmonic structure I am mainly trying to suggest what such models might look like. The best I could hope for is not that my theory would apply throughout the universe of tonal pieces, but that it might provide an example for students of harmonic theory.

It should be obvious that Professor Kraft's statement can be turned around: Progressions of chords imply lines, and the only reason that a line proceeds as it does is that a progression determines its course. If counterpoint books make any sense, it is because they deal with musical motion —that is, harmony. Indeed, but a generation ago this inverted statement might have seemed the more reasonable of the two. The problem with the point of view that this statement reflects is that it overlooks the possibility that a tonal piece may have strong melodic profiles—intervallic spans filled in with step motion, for example—which contribute to our apprehending the piece as a directed and purposeful event succession, and which may be characterizable without reference to the piece's polyphonic context. At the same time, the statement originally quoted expresses a point of view that fails to recognize that some of the patterns inferrable from the chordal partitioning of a tonal piece—patterns of scale-step succession which are diagonal or intralinear, for example—may fail of representation in individual instrumental or registral voices. Moreover, these patterns, while necessarily determined by the manner in which horizontal structures are vertically aligned, may possess a regularity of organization, a systematic nature, which encourages the analyst to consider them as points of departure, as being what the music is about, instead of taking them as the quasi-accidental results of a rhythmic coordination of horizontal structures. Where such coordination is hard to describe, because it is lacking in regularity over a corpus of works or even within a single work, it will seem especially reasonable to start with harmonic progression as a fundamental aspect of coherence.

Characteristic of the present-day tilt toward counterpoint has been a tendency among theorists to rob the term "harmonic progression" of much of its meaning. Taking their cue from the later works of Schenker, many theorists confine their uses of this term to the designation of higher level bass arpeggiations involving the I and V scale-steps. For them a complete harmonic action is the three-pronged affair I–V–I, understood as a succession of bass-line scale-steps and, at the same time, of prolonged triads.

3. "Diatonic circle of fifths" refers here to progressions on the order of I–IV–VII–III–VI–II–V–I.

This point of view has led to some confusion in describing typical constituents of the tonal phrase. Of the IV scale-step Salzer writes, "The IV thus lacks a natural upper-fifth relationship to the I, which considerably weakens its harmonic role. On the other hand, the proximity to V strengthens its driving tendency to this harmony."[4] What is confusing here is that, whereas Salzer is attempting to describe the IV as an element in harmonic progression, he cites its melodic or contrapuntal relation to the V as the primary source of its effect in such progression. It does not seem to occur to him to regard the lower-fifth relationship of IV to the I as the basis of its harmonic meaning, one paralleling that of the I in its relationship to the V. Indeed, the widespread labeling of IV as an agent of dominant preparation testifies to its having become a stepchild in the generative schemes of many theorists, and a curious one at that: Not only is it just tolerated by its unnatural (step-related) parent, the V, as a bit of ceremony enhancing the latter's arrival upon the scene, but its link to its natural (upper-fifth-related) progenitor, the I, goes unacknowledged. One has the feeling that neo-Schenkerians would have less to answer for if the III were to have a more important role in the expression of tonality at immediate levels of structure, but it does not. Rather, it is IV and II that are primary constituents at the level of the phrase and, in many contexts, at the level of the piece as well. A conception of harmonic continuity that accounts for things as they are, at both the level of chord progression and that of key succession, seems desirable to me, and I find that much of contemporary theory has little to offer in this regard. Instead, it is in the theories of Rameau and his followers that such a conception may take historical root. Accordingly, it is their work that serves as inspiration and antecedent for a major component of what follows. At the same time, my decision to employ terms such as "structural level," "contrapuntal transformation," and "fundamental line," not to mention my whole notion of what it means to do analysis and to notate its results, speaks of my sharing in what has become the public debt of our community: the liability incurred in our continuing plunder of Schenker's seemingly inexhaustible legacy. Following a presentation of my own views I will attempt to locate them with respect to these two monuments of the theoretical tradition.

Harmony as Pitch-Class Counterpoint

I will start by making sure that the term "harmony" does not remain "meaningless." I do not intend, by the use of this term, to refer to a textural phenomenon, as in "four-part harmony," a style, as in "chorale har-

---

4. Felix Salzer, *Structural Hearing*, Vol. 1 (New York: Dover, 1962), p. 89.

monization,'' or a pedagogic tool, as in "harmonic dictation''; nor do I have in mind any philosophically extended application of the term along the lines of a *musica humana* or *musica mundana*. Instead, I will use it in a way that rather resembles the Schenkerian use of the term "counterpoint,'' that is, as the name for an underlying level, or series of levels, of musical structure or process in terms of which a musical surface can be heard to cohere. Just as a Schenkerian might choose to hear a passage of tonal music in terms of its underlying species counterpoint, I will speak of hearing pieces in terms of their underlying harmony. In an important sense, though, the two are different, my "harmony" being a degree more abstract than Schenker's "counterpoint": Instances of the latter can be played, even if they have to be speeded up; examples of the former can be played only if their pitch-class (PC) elements are reified as pitches, in which respect they are rather like 12-tone rows.

As I understand it, a harmonic progression is not a succession of vertical complexes so much as it is a counterpoint of lines. What separates such a counterpoint from what we ordinarily call counterpoint is that the lines in a harmonic progression are PC lines. Whereas the structures of traditional counterpoint—such as Fuxian species counterpoint—are defined in pitch-specific terms, the structures of harmony are here, by definition, conceived of in PC terms, that is, without reference to the octave placement or irreducible elements—scale degrees—in an individual harmonic progression. Therefore, whereas traditional counterpoint distinguishes between the bass voice and upper voices, or between perfect fourths and perfect fifths, harmony as I conceive it makes no such distinctions and regards even the matter of melodic contour, so basic to counterpoint, as foreign.

There exists a potential for confusing the harmony of a passage with what I will call its uninterpreted PC representation. The latter is a kind of model arrived at by simply representing each pitch event in the passage by a notational mark that stands for its PC and thereby eliminating the registral profile of the original. This kind of procedure is represented in the first example. The original—the opening measures of Mozart's piano sonata K. 284, III—is given as Example 1.1a, its uninterpreted PC representation as Example 1.1b. A metaphor for what emerges may be had by imagining a keyboard instrument which, upon depression of one of its keys, would sound, not a pitch, but all members of the octave equivalence class of the pitch corresponding to that key that are in the range of audible frequencies.

It should be emphasized that in speaking of harmonic analyses as PC models I am not referring to uninterpreted reductions of this sort. In fact, uninterpreted PC representation is of little use in harmonic analysis since

(a)

(b)

EXAMPLE 1.1

it obliterates registral information on the basis of which harmonic relationships may be sorted out in a given context. The problem with naive reductions of this sort is that they contain pseudo-PCs: misrepresentations of pitches that are of melodic significance only. Necessary components in particular contours of melody, these pitches have no reason for being other than to fill out these contours and, therefore, none apart from the roles they play in their particular octaves.[5]

This distinction between real and apparent or pseudo-PCs is a subtle one. Perhaps the simplest way of getting at it is to go straight to the heart of the matter, namely, the theory that is the subject of this chapter. This approach seems best because the theory is designed to generate models of tonal pieces that contain only their "true" PC content, omitting the rest of what they contain. In other words, the theory is an apparatus by means of which that part of a piece's content that can be described without reference to octave placement can be separated from the part that has no meaning apart from its octave placement. When the theory is understood, and the relationships between its models and particular pieces are grasped, the distinction between true PC and misrepresented pitch will become clear.

Perhaps the most basic premise of this theory is that tonal structure is hierarchial structure in Schenker's sense only to a certain depth and, for

5. For more extended treatment of pseudo-PCs and related matters, see William E. Benjamin, "On Modular Equivalence as a Musical Concept," Dissertation, Princeton, 1976 (Ann Arbor: University Microfilms BRE76-20789), pp. 59–89.

much music, only for piece segments as opposed to entire pieces. With respect to the argument I will develop here, the first of these qualifications is the more important one. What I mean by restricting the depth of application of Schenker-like reduction is that a complete tonal utterance—a phrase, a period, even a short piece—is done a disservice when it is reduced beyond a certain point, to a single triad, say, or to an event succession that is obviously derived from a single triad, such as a Schenkerian *Ursätz*. Instead, I propose to regard such an utterance as being irreducibly founded on an unbroken chain of states, each temporally successive state of which is initiated when some new event(s) is (are) generated from the content of the immediately preceding state. A theory that produces such chains is a collection of rules and other statements that determines the content of the first state, ways of generating events at the nth state from those at the $(n - 1)$th state, and the event-sets that may constitute a state by occupying the position that corresponds to it. Further specifications in the theory may enable a characterization of the chain as a process with beginning, middle, and end, or as one more finely articulated.

The exposition of a theory may be by way of a formal statement of its rule structure or via an informal description of the models it produces. In what follows I proceed informally. Here, then, is a list of important properties of the models of which my theory is capable.

1. Each model is a chain of states. The content of each non-initial state is determined by that of the immediately preceding state, and that of each nonterminal state determines that of each immediately succeeding state.
2. The events of a model are all PCs with one or more diatonic interpretations; that is, they are scale-degrees in one or more major or minor scales. They are not particular pitches.

For complete tonal utterances:

3. The content of the model's initial state is the global tonic triad.
4. Subsequent states, except for the last, may have as their content PC sets with either three or four elements. (If of four PCs these will be major, minor, or diminished triads to which a scale-degree adjacent to and below the triad root has been added. If of three PCs the occupying sets will be tonicized major or minor triads.)
5. The content of the final state is the global tonic triad.

The directed PC interval 5—for example, C to F or E-flat to A-flat, regardless of registral direction—plays a crucial role in linking states of the model because

6. A PC event at state n may spawn another event at state n + 1 if and only if the PC interval from the first to the second is 5. ("To spawn" means here "to be responsible for the generation of without being replaced by or displaced to.")

At the position in the chain at which a newly spawned PC makes its appearance it will necessarily be adjacent, in terms of the operative scale, to at least one already-generated PC. Such adjacencies are valued as unstable and are said to result in scalewise linear displacement of the newly spawned, and not the already-present, PC in one of three ways:

7. PC_1, spawned at state n, lies above and scale-adjacent to PC_2, generated earlier; PC_2 descends to (is displaced to) the next lower scale-degree and does so at state $n + 1$.
8. PC_1, spawned at state n, lies below and scale-adjacent to PC_2, generated earlier; PC_2 ascends to (is displaced to) the next higher scale-degree and does so at state n, that is, simultaneously with the spawning of PC_1. (It may be added here that PC_1 must be PC interval 10 away from—"a whole-step below"—PC_2.)
9. PC_1, spawned at state n, lies below and scale-adjacent to PC_2, generated earlier, and PC_3, destabilized at state $n - 1$, descends at state n (see Statement 7) into the slot into which PC_2 would normally ascend (see Statement 8); PC_2 descends to a PC unison with PC_1 and does so at state n, that is, simultaneously with the spawning of PC_1.

The one exception to these displacement rules occurs when

10. The collection occupying the nth state is a "major–minor seventh chord." In the normal progression to the $(n + 1)$th state the collection that succeeds this one is a (tonicized) triad. To effect this progression the local tonic is spawned from the root of the seventh chord but the third of the seventh chord is upward displaced, as if by virtue of an attraction to the tonic, rather than downward displaced, as implied by Statement 7.

This special behavior of the thirds of major–minor seventh chords allows the event chain to regain triadic stability from time to time and provides a basis, at the PC level, for the phenomenon of cadence.

From the foregoing it is evident that a PC can be generated in one of three ways:

1. It can be there from the beginning as part of the global tonic triad (Statement 3).

2. It can be spawned from a preexistent PC with which it forms PC interval 5 (Statement 6).

3. It can originate in a displacement of a preexistent PC (Statements 7–10).

The theory provides two means whereby modulation is introduced into the system:

11. A state may constitute a transition from one major or minor scale to another if its content belongs in its entirety to both scales.
12. A PC may be chromatically inflected in the progression from one state to the next. Such inflection implies that the chain enters a new scale with the second of these states.

The preceding statements imply particularly strong connections between pairs of events in adjacent states:

13. A PC and the scale-adjacent PC to which it is displaced are called a *linear pair.*[6]
14. A succession of linear pairs such that the first member of each pair (except the first) is at the same time the second member of the preceding pair is called a *line*.
15. The event chain conceived of as a counterpoint of lines is called a *PC counterpoint*.
16. A line in the PC counterpoint that begins on any element of the global tonic triad and terminates on the root of that triad may be called a *fundamental line* of the counterpoint. There may be more than one such line in a counterpoint.

The concept of a fundamental line is important because it defines the end state of the counterpoint as that in which a line reaches its destination. For reasons to be adduced, the fundamental line is not to be equated with Schenker's *Urlinie*.

This completes an informal sketch of the models which PC-counterpoint theory produces. These productions are supposed to capture an underlying aspect of tonal activity that is indifferent, as regards its coherence, to the way it is registrally represented. In other words, the theory views any two octave-equivalent representations of the PC content of any one of its productions (models) as being functionally equivalent. The theory is designed to focus on underlying, and therefore often long-range,

6. The term "linear pair" is borrowed from Arthur Komar, *Theory of Suspensions* (Princeton: Princeton University Press, 1971), p. 14 and pp. 38–43. Komar's concepts are not unrelated to my own but he does not, in my opinion, adequately portray the circumstances under, or ways in which, PC displacement takes place.

structure; it need not stand or fall according to whether it literally reflects or fails to reflect surface events. Still, one finds its plausibility heightened if one is able to observe many short passages of tonal music whose uninterpreted PC representations can be easily transformed into productions of the theory, by virtue, that is, of a transformation apparatus that is simple and relatively unambiguous. Also, precisely because it is about PC structure, the theory becomes still more plausible to the extent that the observed passages are seen to bear nontrivial relationships to the theoretical models to which they correspond, in the sense that PC adjacencies in the models are not represented as pitch adjacencies in the music. Such a nontrivial correspondence is represented in the next two examples.

Example 1.2 shows perhaps the simplest production the theory generates, one which, not unhappily, is well represented in the tonal literature. This example also serves to introduce the analytical notation that subsequent examples will use. The integers under the example identify its five (vertical) states. The initial state shows the tonic triad (Statement 3 above). State 2 results from the spawning of G from the D of State 1 (Statement 6)—indicated by a slur—and the resultant destabilization of F—indicated by the change from white to black notehead—and immediate displacement of A to B-flat (Statement 8). At State 3, F is displaced to E (Statement 7), which in turn destabilizes D. The A at State 4 is spawned from State 3's E and destabilizes State 2's G. At State 4, too, the tonic D is finally displaced to C-sharp the special leading-tone status of which, in the context of State 4's major–minor seventh chord, is signaled by square notation. The final state, at which the tonic triad is regained, is produced

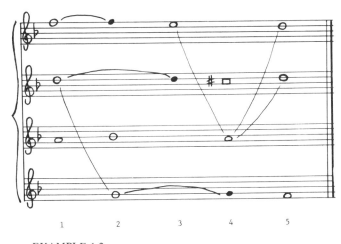

EXAMPLE 1.2

Allegro

EXAMPLE 1.3

by spawning D from A (Statement 6) and thus immediately displacing E (Statement 9) and C-sharp (Statement 10), and G is displaced to F (Statement 7). The fundamental lines of the counterpoint, according to the definition given in Statement 16, are the $\hat{3}-\hat{2}-\hat{1}$ succession F–E–D and the $\hat{1}-\hat{7}-\hat{1}$ succession lying below it in the example.

The excerpt appearing as Example 1.3, mm. 1–3 from Haydn's Opus 76, No. 2, I, bears a clear but nontrivial relationship to the theoretical production given in the preceding example. Except for the fact that States 2 and 3 of the model are collapsed into a single chord at the surface—the $\frac{4}{2}$ sonority in m. 2—the relationship between model and surface is patent. Significantly, the model gives rigorous expression to traditional ways of hearing this and similar passages, according to which there is indeed a stronger connection, in m. 2, between the 'cello's D and second violin's C-sharp than between that D and the 'cello's own succeeding E, and, along similar lines, a link that binds the viola's G (m. 2) to the 'cello's F (m. 3). Importantly, too, the model says something about the inadequacies of traditional harmonic analysis with respect to the most commonplace foregrounds: In Roman numeral analysis some, though not all, of the states in the underlying PC counterpoint are labeled, but the senses in which each state may be said to grow out of the preceding one are not specified.

The model in Example 1.2 presents a harmonic view of the music notated in Example 1.3. Such a view does not deny the existence in the music of an extraharmonic dimension, that is, of contrapuntal structure in a Schenkerian sense. Obviously, the music can be viewed in melodic terms, as a prolongation of the tonic triad in which the chords of m. 2 arise by virtue of passing motions within the prolonged harmony (see Example 1.9 for alternative analytical pictures of the content of mm. 1–4 of this movement). The question is forced on us as to how we are to coordinate these views, if indeed we recognize the validity of each. It is worth bearing in mind that they are not mutually supportive: According to one, the passage is an interpretation of a counterpoint that includes the PC line F–E–D; the other would have it that the governing motion is the pitch line d^1–e^1–f^1 (see Example 1.9). On the face of it this is a contradictory state of affairs and one we avoid facing squarely when we resort to claiming that the passage is, at one and the same time, both these things. Of course it is, but the question then becomes one of priority. Is the music essentially a harmonic construct, the pitch interpretation of which yields a surface structure of registral lines, motives, and the like, or is it essentially a melodic structure exhibiting a subtle trace of harmonic thinking? The bias of contemporary theory is toward the latter interpretation; my own is in the direction of the former, although not especially in cases such as the present one where a few opening measures are under discussion. Basically it is not through the study of isolated fragments that these opposed leanings are best evaluated. This is especially so in the case of the views espoused here, and for this reason: If there is such a thing as a PC line, one that can be defined without reference to register or contour and which can therefore assert itself while traversing a broad pitch spectrum, it is precisely the sort of line one would expect to be operative over broad expanses of musical time; the circumstances binding pitches far removed from one another in terms of frequency, because they bind the PCs these represent, might also be expected to bind representatives of these same PCs that are distant from each other in time. The next section of this essay deals, accordingly, with tonal statements that are longer and, in some senses, complete.

The Theory and Style Analysis

If a music theory is about anything, it is about the things some pieces do that others do not. A properly designed theory, therefore, delimits classes of pieces. The classes thus delimited may be large or small, real or hypothetical, culturally connected or disconnected. Leaving aside questions as to whether a given theory is profound or even consistent, it would appear that it is most interesting if it is one of those that helps to define a repertory that is broadly circumscribed, real, and culturally connected. A theory of this sort is a theory of a musical tradition, and it is of interest to us because it substantiates particular ways of structuring past time as music history.

The theory presented here is among the theories of a particular tradition because it delimits a very large class of pieces composed by Europeans between the late seventeenth century and the present. As such it is necessarily general but, at the same time, appropriately exclusive. The class it defines excludes works that are not fundamentally diatonic—much twentieth-century and some nineteenth-century music. Also excluded are medieval music and neoclassical twentieth-century music because they are nontriadic; most Renaissance music because it is not governed by large-scale descending-fifth progressions; and much music of the early and middle Baroque period because it assigns only nonessential, ornamental functions to seventh chords.

This leaves a large corpus of music including, of course, the Bach to Brahms canon, which is the special focus of Schenker's theory. For each piece in this corpus, the present theory produces a harmonic background in the form of a complex of PC lines. This does not mean that the theory as presented is meant to exhaust what is common to all of these pieces. Of equal generality for this literature are certain conventions with respect to the way these backgrounds are registrally interpreted: Specifically, in all of this music important event-linkages at the PC level, such as those connected with tonicization, are made especially apparent through the manner in which they are presented. The spawnings of new PCs by PC interval 5 are generally consigned to that succession of lowest notes called the bass line, whereas fundamental-line connections are given as pitch adjacencies and often sound in the highest or otherwise most prominent part or, at least, in a home octave. The results of these conventions were posited by Schenker as the starting points of his theory. In my view, there are more basic (PC) structures that function as the operands upon which these conventions work.

Pitch-class counterpoint theory as presented cannot serve on its own to explicate the works to which it is pertinent. It must be used in tandem with a melodic component by means of which pitch interpretations of harmonic backgrounds may be hierarchically, and often recursively, elaborated. No attempt will be made here to describe a set of melodic operations; suffice it to say that, in respect to so vital a component, no contemporary theory can claim to be much more than a tidying up of Schenker's, mine being not even that. In the analyses that follow, the procedures that link a piece's PC background to its pitch surface are obviously Schenker-derived.

Whereas there is much that is common to the accounts that PC-counter-point theory gives of pieces, it is important to consider the different ways in which the theory applies to distinct families of works within the corpus as a whole. These differences do not point to weakness in the theory; on the contrary, if they help to characterize styles more sharply, they may indicate strength. Important differences exist in reference to distinct style families as to (*a*) the rhythmic character of pieces at their PC levels, with particular regard to interruptions and discontinuities in the unfolding of underlying harmonic events; (*b*) the manner in which the PC background is represented, or fails to be represented, as musical surface; (*c*) the extent and nature of chromatic inflection at PC levels; (*d*) the structural value of foreground chord progressions; and (*e*) characteristic melodic procedures by which underlying PC levels are elaborated.

With a view to showing how the theory may be applied, and how it applies differently in differing contexts, there follow some analyses of self-contained, if not complete, tonal utterances. The first work analyzed is perhaps more representative of its composer's instrumental style than it is of any period, however circumscribed. Readers may wish to compare my analysis with the well-known one by Schenker.[7] The succeeding analyses are of shorter stretches of music, which, however, exhibit modes or organization that are extremely typical of the period and place in which they originate.

Analysis of Bach: Largo from the Sonata for Solo Violin in C Minor, BWV 1005

The harmonic background of this composition is given in Example 1.4. The notation in the example has been largely explained but a few symbols added here require explanation. The vertical bars occurring from time to time on the three lower staves—the example contains two four-staff systems beneath each of which there is a summarizing fifth staff—indicate the endings of lines and the beginnings of new lines. Where new lines begin in the middle of the counterpoint their placement on particular staves is, to some extent, arbitrary. Only the top staff contains a piece-spanning line ($\hat{8}-\hat{1}$). The measure numbers above the systems indicate timepoints at which the content of the vertical state aligned with the num-

7. Heinrich Schenker, *Das Meisterwerk in der Musik,* 3 Vols. (Munich: Drei Masken Verlag, 1925, 1926, 1930; reissued as 3 vols. in 1, Hildesheim: Georg Olms, 1974), pp. 63–73. English trans. by John Rothgeb, *Music Forum* IV (New York: Columbia University Press, 1976), pp. 141–59.

ber in question is initiated at the musical surface and begins to be prolonged.

Example 1.4 evinces an aspect, characteristic of the PC levels produced
by the theory, of the ever-presence of a process of generation by PC interval 5. These "spawnings" permeate the PC texture, causing displacement, opening up new lines, and, in the appropriate contexts, promoting
closure. This process of generation is summarized on a fifth staff, below
the actual counterpoint. Included here are a few secondary fifth-relations
(PCs joined by dotted slurs); these may be regarded as the byproducts of
event successions for which the theory has another, perhaps better, explanation. For example, the D in the second state (m. 3) is the result of C's
having been displaced by the spawning of B-flat from F and it is unnecessary to invoke an independent spawning process to explain it.

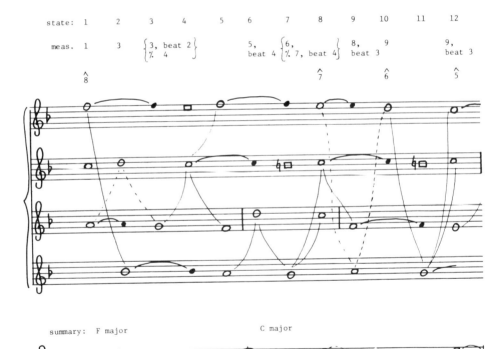

EXAMPLE 1.4

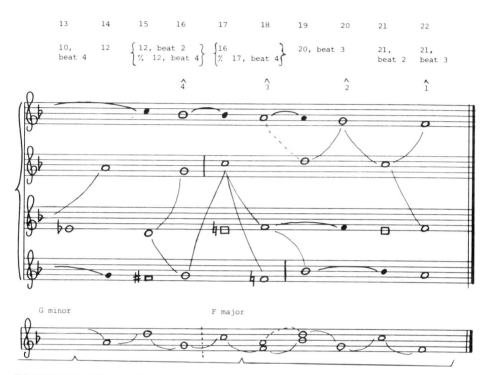

EXAMPLE 1.4 (*Continued*)

Were Schenker to regard the summary that underlies this contrapuntal model, he might well ascribe to it that same aspect of perpetual motion he sees as a negative characteristic of Rameau's tonal models.[8] The summary itself does appear to be chasing its own tail without reflecting in any way what makes the end of the piece more than just the end of another diatonic fifth-cycle. What this criticism would be missing, however, is the context of nonrecurrence in which the fifth-cycle ostinato takes on fresh significance with each reappearance. This context includes the large-scale

8. Heinrich Schenker, "Rameau oder Beethoven? Erstarrung oder geistiges Leben in der Musik," *Das Meisterwerk in der Musik*, III, p. 13. English trans. by Sylvan Kalib, "Thirteen Essays from the Three Yearbooks *Das Meisterwerk* . . . by Heinrich Schenker: An Annotated Translation," Dissertation, Northwestern, 1973, vol. 2, p. 496.

key succession, most palpable as a rhythm of tonicizing cadences that forms a temporal counterpoint to the rhythm of fifth-cycle recurrence, as the example shows. Even more important, however, is the noncyclic content of the actual PC lines themselves. The fundamental line is an $\hat{8}-\hat{1}$ "descent"; this is a piece-spanning, and therefore nonrecurring, pattern. It is worth examining in relation to the octave *Urlinie*, which Schenker posits as fundamental to this piece. An important difference between the two is a rhythmic one: Schenker's moves, from $\hat{8}$ to $\hat{7}$, $\hat{7}$ to $\hat{6}$, and so on, occur in quite different places. A second difference lies in the relative complexity of the lines in my model when compared with his *Urlinien* in general: My PC lines may contain reversals of direction that are understood as part of their essential, irreducible content. Also, secondary tonal content (change of scale) is, as I shall show, a necessary feature of my lines, whereas it is excluded from Schenker's.

The source of these differences is clearly identifiable. In Schenker's theory there is basically no concept of displacement; *Urlinie* descent is not tied to particular harmonic or tonal circumstances, whether of fifth-progression, dissonance between background elements (which cannot arise with Schenker), or leading-tone disposition. It is often loosely based on things like these, but not consistently and certainly not explicitly so. A Schenker *Urlinie* is supposed to represent an ideal listener's unified grasp of the essential content of an actual piece-spanning complex of surface melody. Unfortunately, when the melodies being analyzed are as complex as Bach's, the number of nonidentical ideal listeners turns out to be quite astonishing, leaving any one of them, including Schenker, open to the charge of arbitrariness. While the present theory makes no advance toward the probably undesirable goal of finding the best analysis of any piece, it does considerably restrict the conditions under which displacement, or essential motion of an underlying voice, can take place. It says, for example, that, corresponding to one descending-fifth progression, there can be only one displacement in any PC line. This makes Schenker's analysis of the Largo, in which the $\hat{8}-\hat{7}-\hat{6}-\hat{5}$ descent takes place in mm. 7–8 over a V–I bass motion, impossible. Perhaps more interestingly, my theory specifies that certain displacements are impossible under any conditions and others unlikely in certain tonal circumstances. For example, the displacement $\hat{7}-\hat{6}$ cannot occur unless the $\hat{7}$ is reinterpreted as $\hat{3}$ in the dominant scale. Therefore, $\hat{7}-\hat{6}-\hat{5}$ in the "octave" line of Example 4 is really, and necessarily, $\hat{3}-\hat{2}-\hat{1}$ in C major. The next displacement in that line, nominally $\hat{5}-\hat{4}$ in F major, can be executed in the global tonic scale, but only with some difficulty if the tonicized dominant triad is the point of departure as it is here (m. 9, beat 3). The problem is that the succession of events needed to generate $\hat{5}-\hat{4}$ in the tonic scale, given this starting point, is precisely that needed to generate, and just previously employed to generate, $\hat{8}-\hat{7}$ in the dominant scale, as Example 1.5 shows. Whereas this does not demand a modulation to the scale of II or to that of IV to bring about $\hat{5}-\hat{4}$ in a convincing way, it certainly does suggest it. The usefulness of PC-counterpoint theory in accounting for the modulatory structure of pieces is a feature not shared by Schenker's theory. For him, the basic structures of tonality, the *Ursätze* and the middlegrounds derived from these, are obscured by modulation and other, lower forms of dissonance.

An analysis which begins with a PC counterpoint moves toward the surface of an actual piece by showing, as its next stage, the primary melodic or registral interpretation of this counterpoint. In Example 1.6 there appears such an interpretation with respect to part of the PC counterpoint appearing in Example 1.4. An explanation of the notation employed in Example 1.6 is in order. All white noteheads are pitch interpretations of PCs appearing in Example 1.4. Large black noteheads are the pitch correspondents of unstable, about-to-be-displaced PCs that appear as black noteheads in Example 1.4. The small black noteheads in Example 1.6 do not correspond to anything in Example 1.4; they are elements of purely melodic significance—such as passing and neighbouring tones—that constitute a first layer of characteristic melodic substance out of which springs the surface motivic content of the composition. Solid slurs connect white noteheads to large black noteheads and merely reproduce the slurs in Example 1.4. Dotted slurs are a kind of visual aid: They connect multiple surface appearances of an undisplaced harmonic element (white

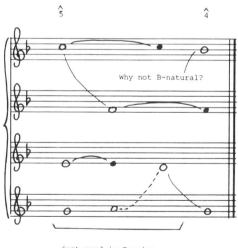

EXAMPLE 1.5

EXAMPLE 1.6

notehead). Diagonal beams connect the pitch representations of PC elements that are PC interval 5 apart and the first of which is thought of as spawning the second; where such a beam is dotted, a nonessential fifth-relation is identified. Straight lines are used to trace the progress of PC lines from one register to another. Leading tones are once again indicated with square notation.

Parentheses are used in Example 1.6 to identify sections of music that elaborate, trope, and in a sense interrupt, more fundamental and "necessary" continuities of musical thought—subordinate clauses, as it were. They correspond to the curly brackets on the measure-number line in Example 1.4. The latter enclose segments of the PC counterpoint that occur twice in the actual music, as indicated by the repeat signs within them. Example 1.6 shows exactly what was intended at Example 1.4. In a way that is extremely typical of Bach's style, the harmonic content of each tonicization—specifically, each tonic triad and the state or pair of states preceding it in Example 1.4—is presented twice in Example 1.6. The first presentation is a "weaker" one in that governing fifth-relations are scattered about the upper voices; the second, in which at least the final tonic-reaching fifth-relation is presented as an easy-to-grasp succession of lowest tones, forms the cadence proper. Schenker avails himself of a similar notion of background events happening twice in his formulation of the concept of *Unterbrechung*,[9] usually translated as "Interruption." He also encloses sections of his foreground sketches in parentheses, as in the analysis of this Largo, but he in no way links this practice to the Interruption concept. For him, Interruption is appropriately invoked only in the context of large-scale thematic parallelism, and he does not make use of it in his analyses of Bach's binary forms. In Schenker's view, the music contained between the first set of parentheses in Example 6 is of contrapuntal origin and continues to prolong the tonic sonority introduced in m. 1. In my view, it is counterintuitive to regard the content of m. 3 as anything other than a prefiguring of the cadential action in m. 4.

The square brackets in Example 1.6 surround PC elements that have been suppressed. For example, the g^1, b^1 dyad on the fourth beat of m. 7 is understood as an incomplete dominant seventh chord. Suppression of background sevenths, as Rameau so remarkably grasped, is a particularly common feature of tonal foregrounds, although not so characteristic of the late Baroque as it is of the Classical style.

---

9. Heinrich Schenker, *Neue musikalische Theorien und Phantasien*, Vol. III, *Der freie Satz* (Vienna: Universal Edition, 1935), p. 65 ff; trans. into English under the title *Free Composition* and newly edited and annotated by Ernst Oster (New York: Longman, 1979), p. 36 ff.

Also included in Example 1.6, on the single staff above the two-staff system, is a tracing of one of the many possible long-range paths through its content. This shows a pairing of large-scale melodic motives: a rising arpeggiation motive (''X'') is complemented by a descending scale motive (''Y''). The first of these is then repeated a tone higher, which ''implies'' complementation by Y, also a tone higher. This implication is realized, in a minor key transformation, just before the G minor cadence. It is important to understand that large-scale melodies of this kind are not background melodies. Certainly they are not necessarily such on account of their large time scale, and what rules them out as such is that they are made up of elements drawn from different levels of structure. What they are, quite simply, are nice things to hear, patterns that contribute to the special quality of a piece. Their creation, not that of fundamental PC lines, presupposes the exercise of a significant composer's imagination.

A Mozart Example and One by Haydn

The most striking difference, at the level of underlying structure, between late Baroque and Classical instrumental music is a rhythmic one. The Bach example just discussed is stylistically representative in this respect: Its background is unfolded with comparative durational regularity. This is not to say that it is metrically uniform at this level; it is just that no harmonic state is represented by a particularly lengthy stretch of music and none by a particularly brief one. The extent of backtracking is minimal: Short segments of harmonic material are repeated as a means of key stabilization, but these repetitions are disguised at the surface. Furthermore, the continuity of harmonic process is not interrupted by longish sections of an exclusively melodic nature; there are no composed-out harmonic *fermati*. The overall result is of smooth, unimpeded linear flow. The Mozart excerpt analyzed in Example 1.7—the variation theme from the third movement of the piano sonata, K. 284—provides a contrast to the Bach on all these counts. Here we have a theme in four phrases. The final phrase interprets the harmonic background in its entirety and without interruption. It is not merely the completing phrase of the piece, but a complete run-through of the piece's essential (harmonic) content. The three earlier phrases express a complex rhythmic process in which the underlying harmonic flow is initiated, its completion withheld but prefigured, and its progress brought to a standstill, whereupon a melodic process takes over which, remarkably, is both a ''left-to-right'' tracing of the basic path just traveled and a ''right-to-left'' transition back to that path's starting point.

The PC and primary-pitch models of this music are given in Examples

1.7a and 1.7b, respectively. By reading these concurrently and referring to the score a sense of the complex rhythmic relationship between phrase structure and underlying harmonic process may be gained. The first phrase carries the fundamental PC line from its point of origin ($\hat{5}$) to a mid-way point ($\hat{3}$) reached in m. 3. As Example 1.7b shows, however, the

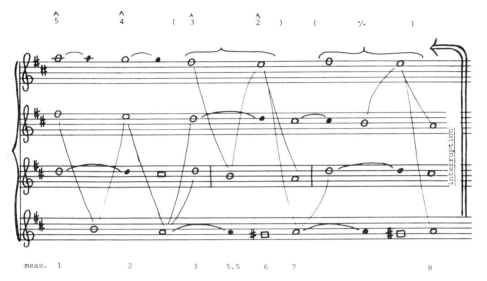

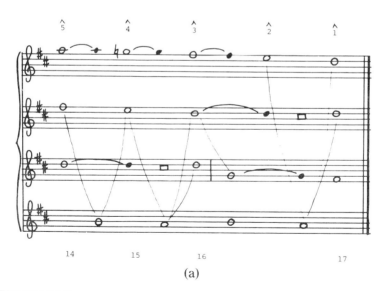

(a)

EXAMPLE 1.7

meas. 1   2   3   4   5

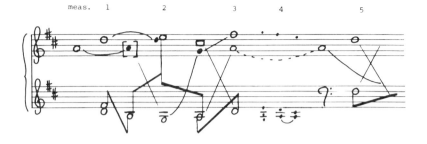

6   7   8

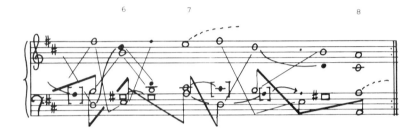

9   10   11   12

14   15   16   17

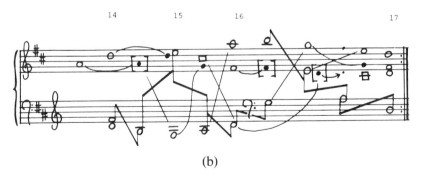

(b)

EXAMPLE 1.7 (*Continued*)

structural upper-register pitch line for this passage is the rising d^2-e^2-f-sharp^2. The events of mm. 3–4 are represented in Example 1.7b but not in Example 1.7a; this means that they are accorded melodic, but not harmonic, significance. To be of harmonic significance the V in m. 4 would have to be either an explicit or implicit dominant seventh chord or a tonicized dominant triad. It is obviously not the latter, and while it might be heard as the former—a G might be imagined on, say, the second quarter of m. 4—it is only by violating its character as the point of rest of an imperfect cadence that it could so be heard. In effect, then, the cadence ending the first phrase is a stylistically typical melodic interruption of the harmonic process. Half-cadential interruptions often serve to prefigure analogous moves on the PC level; in this case, the move from $\hat{3}$ to $\hat{2}$, which occurs at the start of the second phrase, in mm. 5–6, is prefigured. After effecting the true displacement of the $\hat{3}$, the second phrase is occupied with filling out a four-measure time-span complementary to that of the first phrase. In mm. 7–8 there is a $\hat{3}-\hat{1}$ descent in A major that likewise foreshadows later events, namely those of the final measures, but the second phrase takes the fundamental line no further than $\hat{2}$.

The next phrase, mm. 9–13, is interpreted in Example 1.7b as a melodic elaboration of the V reached in m. 7 and confirmed in m. 8, one which reduces to the conventional figure-bass formula $^{6-5}_{4-3}$. The melodic working out is particularly interesting here: The down–up, down–up arpeggiation motive which spans mm. 7–9 (a^2-f-sharp^2, f-sharp$^2-d^2$) is transposed a perfect fourth up and embedded within itself in m. 10. The pitch motion from a^2 to e^2 that spans the phrase as a whole is easily heard as retracing the PC descent accomplished in the first two phrases. At the same time, the chromatic shifts in m. 9 reintroduce the tonic scale and prepare for a resumption of the PC process at its point of origin. In the final phrase PC developments in the first two phrases are recapitulated, and the process is completed without further interruption.

It may be asked whether harmonic processes are themselves hierarchical; whether, that is, harmonic activity in tonal pieces is more than simply a flat background that is filled out melodically. The answer for pieces of any length, and especially for pieces in Classical style, appears to be in the affirmative. Consider, for example, the opening of phrase 3 from the Mozart theme, given in Example 1.8a. In the foregoing remarks this stretch of foreground was given a nonharmonic interpretation. Quite clearly, however, it can also be heard as representing the harmonic process modeled in Example 1.8b. What clarifies this is a lower-level, or secondary, harmonic process with respect to the content of Example 1.7a is that the former is not harmonically continuous with that which would precede it if it were inserted into the latter at the appropriate place. Specifically, the PC events represented at the start of m. 9 (Example 1.8b) can-

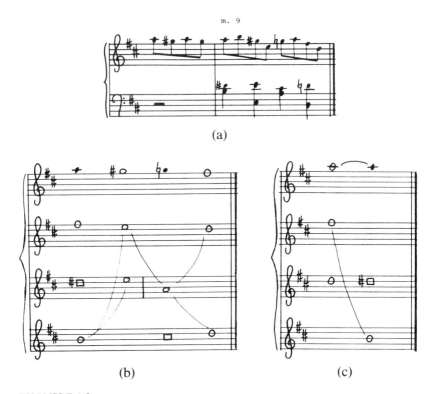

EXAMPLE 1.8

not follow as a next state from those represented at m. 8 (Example 1.7a) according to the theory advanced here. Interestingly enough, they could follow upon a preceding state occupied by a tonic triad, as Example 1.8c shows. It would hardly be appropriate to begin the second half of the theme in this way because of the resulting back-to-back placement of a phrase-terminating tonicized V and an unprepared phrase-initiating I, but the required transitional phrase, here the third, need not be heard as a melodic prolongation of V; instead, it can be heard as a harmonic anticipation of I. Both interpretations recognize discontinuity in the third phrase and both agree that an interruption and return takes place in mm. 12–14, but the orthodox view of this phrase as a V prolongation misses the discontinuity between the second and third phrases and the an-ticipatory value of the secondary harmonic process in m. 9.

The question as to where harmonic process ends and melodic process takes over is not one to be resolved theoretically. Analysts will differ in their applications of a theory that generates descriptions but does not prescribe ways of attaching these to musical objects. What can be said, of course, is that the present theory does specify harmonic connectedness as the basis of underlying structure and melodic prolongation as a filling-out process. This does not mean, however, that harmonic process is necessarily long-range. It is a feature of all tonal pieces, and especially of Classical works, that their structural depth is time-variant: At places in any tonal piece the structure as a whole becomes shallow, with the result that deep- and surface-level phenomena become one. Ultimately, there are analytical choices to be made, on grounds which, in part, must be extra-theoretical. Consider once again the opening phrase of Haydn's "*Quinten*" quartet, this time in its entirety. A pitch-contrapuntal account, such as is given in Example 1.9a, portrays the phrase as a way of melodically

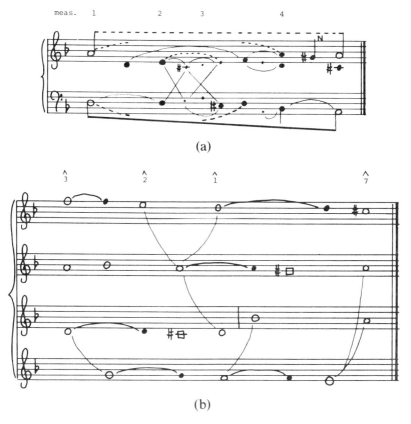

(a)

(b)

EXAMPLE 1.9

unfolding I and connecting it to an interrupting or "dividing" V. The PC-contrapuntal account given in Example 1.9b, however, shows a harmonic process in nine stages by virtue of which an incomplete fundamental line F–C-sharp is generated. Thinking in PC terms, and from the standpoint of the movement as a whole, the harmonic process this first phrase is shown by Example 1.9b to embody is one of secondary or local significance. The deepest-level harmonic process is occupied with the fundamental-line descent from $\hat{5}$, and not with one from $\hat{3}$.

Example 1.10 makes this clear. The harmonic process underlying the development section of this movement may also be seen here and is of considerable interest. It consists of two event-chains by which the F-major triad with which the exposition ends is connected first to the A-major triad in m. 72 and later to the V7 in m. 98. Both chains displace the fundamental line's F to E, but the provisional or preparatory nature of the first chain is made evident at the surface by the absence of E from the cadential chord at m. 72.

Some interesting relationships in this movement between harmonic background and musical surface are worthy of mention. The first harmonic state occupied by (B-flat, D, F, A)—State 6a in Example 1.10—stands for a stretch of music (mm. 63–71, beat 3) in which no seventh chord containing these four PCs actually appears on the surface. Instead, there is a sequential surface progression from a B-flat major triad (mm. 63–64) to a D minor triad (mm. 67–71). Taken together, these two triads

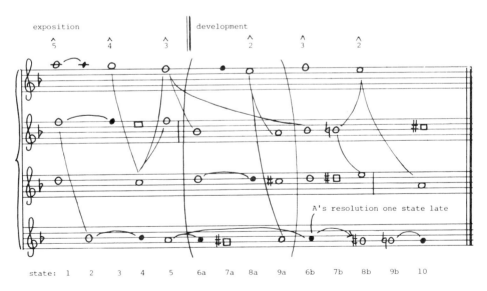

EXAMPLE 1.10

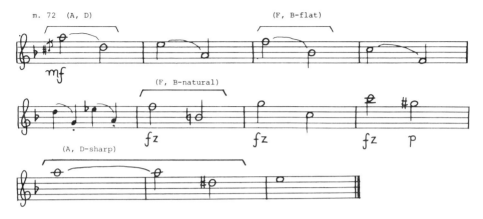

EXAMPLE 1.11

jointly represent State 6 of the PC counterpoint. The surface representation of the progression from State 6b to state 7b (Example 1.10) is especially subtle. Neither of the PC sets involved—(B-flat, D, F, A) and (B-natural, D-sharp, F, A)—is present as a chord at the surface, but the motion from one to the other is clearly what the first-violin melody in mm. 72–81 is, in an important sense, about, as Example 1.11 shows.

Summary

If the musical excerpts studied here are stylistically typical, we may be justified in comparing Bach's instrumental style to that of the Viennese Classicists on the following counts.

1. With respect to rhythm and continuity: Bach's surfaces represent their backgrounds with little interruption and at an even rate of flow; in Mozart and Haydn background flow is frequently interrupted, and harmonic progression occurs at a much less even rate and in a way that incorporates many types of discontinuity.

2. As regards the representation of the background at the surface: Bach's surfaces represent most of their underlying harmonies as simultaneities; in Mozart's and Haydn's music, underlying seventh chords are often not given literal representation at the surface.

3. With respect to the extent of chromaticism at the background: There is considerable use of chromatic inflection or shift as a mode of underlying harmonic connection in Classical pieces; in Bach's music the use of this technique is considerably more restricted. Perhaps the most obvious man-

ifestation of this distinction lies in the relative ubiquity of background augmented-sixth chords in Classical contexts.

4. Concerning the nature of surface chord progression: Chord progressions generated by melodic activity are generally easier to spot in Bach's music than in Mozart's or Haydn's. There are considerable stretches of foreground in Bach's music that show no influences of descending-fifth progression in the succession from one chord to the next. In Mozart's and Haydn's music the surface is seldom free of any influence of harmonic thinking; even where a melodic explanation is more plausible, an alternative explanation, in harmonic terms, may be possible.

A fifth point of comparison, noted earlier, would be in regard to the melodic component itself. It is certain that there are fundamental differences between these styles with respect to techniques of melodic prolongation and motivic organization on various time scales. Melodic structure is, however, a much less systematic affair than harmony, and a piece can be described as being melodically coherent from a great many points of view, none of which has been explicitly presented here. For this reason, I do not feel justified in making this sort of comparison at this point.

The Theory and Other Theories

Tonal theory as bequeathed to us by earlier generations is largely the work of Rameau and Schenker, the original contributions of a host of lesser figures notwithstanding. Although major advances in theory construction and analytical technique have occurred in recent years, and important contributions have been made toward a theory of tonal rhythm, no more adequate theory of the nature of tonal coherence has been propounded than that inferrable from the writings of these two great individuals. My own work is largely an attempt to develop aspects of the thought of each along lines that promote a reconciliation of their apparently divergent viewpoints.

It is more than a little unfair to Rameau to compare him with Schenker. Whereas Schenker could view the tonal tradition retrospectively, Rameau set himself the task of describing the grammar of a language state that had only just crystallized. One would hardly expect his theory to have attained the explanatory scope of a theory formulated so long after the fact. A common misconception regarding Rameau is that he was a strict verticalist interested only in the labeling of chords. He was nothing of the kind, of course. His principal aim was to demonstrate that a tonal piece could be modeled as a succession of vertical states that progresses horizontally according to certain rules. Each succession of two underlying states his rule system can generate is called a cadence, and each cadence type has features that distinguish it from arbitrary chord progressions that are not cadential. The most important of these features are (*a*) a generating or motivating scale-degree succession to which Rameau gives the name "fundamental bass," and (*b*) a characteristic pattern of dissonance (in the first vertical state) followed by resolution (in the second).

As Allan Keiler has pointed out,[10] Rameau's fundamental bass has often been criticized as a poor précis of musical actualities when it was never intended as such a précis but rather as a summary of the underlying conditions that determine particular sets of actualities and through which apparently different sets of actualities may be identified with one another. When Rameau explains the succession I–II$_5^6$–V–I by way of the *double emploi*, he is not claiming that the II$_5^6$ has two successive bass tones; rather, he is encouraging us to hear it as strongly determined by the preceding I and as strongly determining the succeeding V and is saying that to hear it in both these ways is to hear it as two different things. There is nothing primitive about this thinking. What is primitive about Rameau is his metalanguage: The fundamental bass is nothing but an unfortunate adaptation of the traditional figured bass. Conditioned as he was by the intellectual and musical traditions of his time, it was impossible for Rameau not to portray his most original theoretical construct as a mere succession of acoustic roots underlying a musical texture and thus to reify it as some sort of imaginary bass line. What he seems to have been trying to conceptualize, however, is something much more powerful: a governing PC line that would be seen to control the motions of other PC lines by acting as a displacing agent. His own words give vivid expression to this notion:

> Que fait de son côté la B. F? [basse fondamentale] elle vient heurter, pour ainsi dire, une consonance, la rend dissonante, & la force de s'éloigner d'elle en descendant: tout est *préparé* & *sauvé* par ce moyen, toûjours sans qu'on y pense. J'ai tiré une ligne entre cette consonance & la même note rendue dissonante par le choc qu'elle reçoit be sa B. F.[11]

10. Allan Keiler, "On the Sources and Interpretation of Analytic Vocabulary in the History of Music Theories: the Case of Rameau's Fundamental Bass," paper presented to the national conference of the Society for Music Theory, held in Minneapolis, Minnesota, in October 1978.

11. "[What in turn does the fundamental bass do? It hurtles itself, so to speak, against a consonant tone, transforms the latter into a dissonant one, and forces it to move away by descending: Everything is prepared and resolved in this way, without one's ever having to be conscious of it. I have drawn a line between this consonant tone and the same tone made dissonant by the shock received from its fundamental bass.]" J.-P. Rameau, *Code de musique pratique* (Paris: Imprimerie Royale, 1760); facsimile edition in *Monuments of Music and Music Literature*, second series, vol. V (New York: Broude Bros., 1965), p. 33.

Although the expression "PC model" was not part of Rameau's meta-language, it is obvious on page after page of the Traité, the Code, and other works that he was essentially interested in isolating and describing those aspects of tonal coherence that are independent of particular registral interpretation. It is these aspects which, for him, constitute harmony; the melodic aspects he relegates to the categories of "good taste" and "license." These words, on the subject of the perfect cadence, are typical:

> We may choose as many parts as we wish to use together, and place them in any desired order. Those parts found above may be placed below, etc. Only the fundamental bass cannot naturally change its position, although even it is free from constraint as long as good taste guides us. To avoid a perfect conclusion, it may be placed in an upper part, while the bass [*continuo*] proceeds diatonically.[12]

My deep indebtedness to Rameau will be obvious to informed readers. My summaries of generation by PC interval 5 (see Example 1.4) are merely instances of a type of fundamental bass of which Rameau, and followers like Kirnberger and Sechter, was particularly fond. As is the case with Rameau, my vertical states, with the exception of local and global tonic triads, are dissonant.[13] Like Rameau, too, I describe harmony as voice-leading of a necessary kind, which underlies the contingent voice-leading of instrumental and registral parts. While following Rameau to this extent, I try to avoid repeating his errors, which are legion. So as not to dwell unnecessarily on these here, I can simply say that Rameau's principal fault lay in his mistaken notion that every surface chord represents an underlying harmonic state. His failure to appreciate the full scope of the melodic process and essentially nonimmediate (noncontiguous at the surface) nature of the harmonic process limited him to cumbersome accounts of musical surfaces that often seem more in need of explication than the surfaces themselves.

As it is with Rameau's shortcomings, so it is with Schenker's strengths: They are many and well-known. I have already commented on some of the differences between Schenker's conception of underlying structure and my own, and on similarities in our conceptions of surface structure. I find, as others have, that it is difficult to pin down Schenker as having been committed to this or that notion since his ideas were in constant flux.

---

12. Rameau, *Treatise on Harmony*, translated from the French (*Traité de l'harmonie*, 1722) with an introduction and notes by Philip Gossett (New York: Dover, 1971), p. 70. The brackets are Gossett's.

13. *Ibid.*, p. 83, where the following appears: "in all progressions of a descending fifth or an ascending fourth (which are the same), the first sound may and even should bear a seventh chord."

His view of harmony appears to have undergone particularly extensive revision over the course of a long creative career. He begins as a proponent of nineteenth-century scale-step theory, which he extends in highly imaginative ways. At its most extended, Schenker's version of this theory may be summarized as one that posits that, in their broad designs, phrases, sections, and even entire tonal pieces are governed by canonical progressions of diatonic scale-degrees, the sonic representation of which varies considerably from case to case. Favored among these progressions is the diatonic circle of fifths, and it is Schenker's heavy reliance on this construct and its derivatives that constitutes his principal link to the Rameau tradition. Piece- or section-spanning cycles of the form I–IV–VII–III–VI–II–V–I persist in Schenker's output up to and including the *Meisterwerk* yearbooks.[14] It is also at about this time, however, that the *Urlinie* concept crystallizes in his work. Instead of attempting to reconcile the two, as I have tried to do here, Schenker begins to lose interest in canonical scale-step progressions and more and more comes to regard the *Urlinie* as shaping the course of a lengthy tonal utterance. Since, in Schenker's view, the *Urlinie* is a pitch construct, one with a particular registral position and contour in each piece, he begins to take less and less interest in those aspects of tonal coherence that are register-independent. By the time of *Der freie Satz*, even the *bassbrechung*, which is regarded primarily as supportive of, and in this sense secondary to, the *Urlinie*, is described as having a proper (rising, then falling) contour and, to this extent, described as a melodic phenomenon.[15] In his later work, Schenker regards tonal music as thoroughly contrapuntal. Harmonic states are the sometimes necessary, sometimes arbitrary by-products of melodic transformations of an underlying structure that is itself the product of melodic impulses.

The mechanisms of transformation in Schenker's theory are too well known to be entered into here. Characteristic of his analyses is the application of the same mechanisms at every level of structure. This results in a situation in which the listener is ultimately asked to hear any stretch of music identified as a functional segment in a Schenker analysis as taking part in the prolongation of one of three background collections, an initial tonic, a medial dominant, and a final tonic. I find this situation an uncomfortable one because it forces an assignment of structural weight to musical events and event-classes in ways I regard as distortive. Schenker will,

14. See the analysis of Bach's Little Prelude, No. 7, in Schenker, *Das Meisterwerk in der Musik*, I, p. 107.
15. H. Schenker, *Der freie Satz* (1935), part 1, sect. 2, ch. 3, "Von der Bassbrechung im Allgemeinen," p. 36.

for example, typically regard a passage that begins with a tonicized V, proceeds by elaborately tonicizing VI, IV, or II, or some combination of these, and continues with a return to the tonic scale, finally ending up on the dominant seventh chord, as constituting in its entirety a prolongation of V. This interpretation fails to capture the sense in which the tonicized V represents departure from, and the V7 return to, the tonic, and it both undervalues the intervening tonicizations and fails to adequately account for their role in neutralizing ''departure from'' and thus promoting ''return to.'' Indeed, the very notions of ''departure from'' and ''return to'' are foreign to Schenkerian thinking. They do not seem to me to be foreign to most tonal music.

Returning to what I said at the start, the basic difference between Schenker's view and my own is that I do not believe, as he does, that chord prolongation is an operative force below a certain depth of tonal structure. If it were, in my view, chord progressions and key successions would be as idiosyncratic to particular pieces as other, universally acknowledged aspects of melodic design such as motives, themes, and various long- and short-range pitch lines. This, however, is not the case. Instead, chord succession is virtually canonical throughout the repertory, and key succession is quite uniform for certain styles. Also, for Schenker to be able to say that underlying structure holds together in the same ways as surface structure, he must deny that key successions are to the middleground as chord progressions are to the foreground, since it is obvious that key successions do not duplicate chord successions under any reasonable interpretation. I know of very few pieces with the key scheme I–IV–V–I.[16] I find uncomfortable the necessity to deny what seems to me an obvious correspondence, to say the least.

In attempting better to account for what appear to me to be the actualities of tonal music, its ordered progressions of chords and keys, I make use of the prolongation concept, but only at levels relatively close to the musical surface. Underlying the voice-leading structures of a tonal composition there are, I submit, deeper layers of structure at which prolongation no longer operates. At these layers events displace and depart from one another in a controlled process which is calculated to insure that what was departed from will return in a convincing way.

---

16. An interesting exception that proves the rule is the keyboard Concerto in D minor, W. 23, by C. P. E. Bach. The first movement has four extended ritornello statements occurring successively in D minor, G minor, A minor, and D minor. This is published in Arnold Schering, editor (1906) and Hans Joachim Moser, editor of the revised edition (1958), *Denkmäler deutscher Tonkunst*, Vols. 29–30 (Wiesbaden: Breitkopf & Härtel, and Graz: Akademische Druck- und Verlagsanstalt, 1958), p. 62.

2

Barney Childs

POETIC AND MUSICAL RHYTHM: ONE MORE TIME

As Jane R. Stevens points out, "Musical rhythm . . . appears to be receiving a renewed burst of attention,"[1] citing the books by Cooper and Meyer, Yeston, and Seidel; to these can of course be added several recent articles and reviews. Few writing on the topic omit at least passing mention, often including discussion at length, of the analogies of musical and poetical rhythm, usually invoking the classical apparatus for scansion of poetry and in some cases appropriating this for analysis of music. I suggest that a clarification of this material may be of assistance through a brief resumé, a mention of what appear to me to be misconceptions concerning the application of one criterion of classification to another, and, finally, comment upon recent approaches in music and poetry in which the traditional rhythmic hierarchies are replaced, altered, or eliminated.[2]

Prosody, Rhythm, and Meter

Any prosody with which I am familiar develops means of ordering certain sound features natural to the language in which the poetry is written as well as the codification of these means. In the Western world, the

1. Review of William Seidel, *Rhythmus: Eine Begriffsbestimmung, Journal of Music Theory* 21.2 (Fall 1977), 382. Music periodicals in this listing will be referred to by their bibliographic abbreviations. *JMT: Journal of Music Theory. PNM: Perspectives of New Music. ITO: In Theory Only. Proc. ASUC: Proceedings of the American Society of University Composers. MQ: Musical Quarterly.*

2. Part of this essay has been reworked from an earlier presentation. "Articulation in Sound Structures: Some Notes toward an Analytic," *Texas Studies in Literature and Language* VII:3 (Fall 1966), 423–45. Some of the material here appears there in more detail.

33

poet's direction in this ordering has consistently been with *measure,* a concern that has been extensive since classical times. Greek and Roman poetic theory arranged measure in terms of long and short syllables, these to be assembled in various combinations to make up the working unit of the poetic foot. Feet, in turn, were assembled to provide the poetic line. In England, however, an alteration of this tradition resulted from the confluence, post-Conquest, of the Continental extension of the classical use of syllable length[3] and the Scandinavian-German-based "native tongue," Old English, this drawing upon arrangement of stress or accent to provide the patterns of measure. The resulting mixture took some time, close to 500 years, to even itself out. We can illustrate this by looking at, first, a few lines of Old English poetry, each made up of two half-lines, each of these organized around two strong accents:

> *Mæg ic be me sylfum   soðgied wrecan,*
> *si þas secgan,   hu ic geswincdagum*
> *earfoðhwile   oft þrowade,*
> *bitre breostceare   gebiden hæbbe,*
> *gecunnad in ceole   cearselda fela,*
> *atol y þa gewealc.*

—THE SEAFARER

second, some lines from the late fourteenth-century *Sir Gawain and the Green Knight,* still retaining the four powerful accents but regularizing the syllable-weight order to some degree and generally extending the foot:

> *For werre wrathed hym not so much, þat wynter was wors,*
> *When þe colde cler water fro þe cloude₃ schadde,*
> *And fres er hit falle my₃t to þe fale erþe;*
> *Ner slayn with þe slete he sleped in his yrnes*
> *Mo ny₃te₃ þen innoghe in naked rokke₃. . . .*

and third, Chaucer's verse, influenced by French and Italian models, in which the classical foot and syllable-counting have become the ordering principle *with stress replacing length.*[4]

> *The bisy larke, messager of the day,*
> *Salueth in hir song the morwe gray,*
> *And firy Phebus riseth up so bright*

---

3. Latin verse by this time had of course already begun to absorb rhythmic features of various native languages. Cf. William Beare, *Latin Verse and European Song* (London: Methuen, 1957).

4. For a coherent discussion of the Renaissance fusion of the two traditions of English poetry cf. Douglas L. Peterson, *The English Lyric from Wyatt to Donne* (Princeton: Princeton University Press, 1967).

That al the orient laugheth of the light,
And with his stremes dryeth in the greves
The silver dropes hangynge on the leves.

—CANTERBURY TALES

An important point here is that although the scansion—the notation, if you will—of the movement of English poetry originally retained the marking of long and short syllables by the classical — and ⌣ , what came to be so marked were stressed and unstressed syllables, finally more accurately indicated ′ and ⌣ . No reputable prosodist today uses the older markings, those of length and quantity, for a body of poetry which is accentually ordered.

The appropriation of the diacritics of poetic scansion, of the poetic feet themselves, for application in discussion of musical rhythm, has apparently been accepted by musical scholarship for many years. When Cooper and Meyer,[5] for example, provide their list of the five feet basic to musical rhythm (iamb, anapest, trochee, dactyl, and amphibrach), these acceptably to establish patterns of strong and weak beats,[6] they use the symbols for length (−⌣) rather than stress (′⌣). This may have honorable historical precedence from a tradition of past German musical scholarship, but it is still flatly inaccurate. The problem of agogic accent in music, of the relationship of duration to stress, is complex enough without the imprecision and confusion that retention of this notation can produce.

What we have available in English-language poetry is actually a fourfold choice in ordering sound.

1. Quantitative poetry, in which movement is organized through arrangement of long and short syllables. About the only plausible attempt to devise a quantitative prosody for English was that of Thomas Campion, but an occasional mention of it can be found today.[7] Purely quantitative means to organize music on the classical model had its last workable solution with the composers of the Academie Baïf.

2. Accentual poetry, the direct descendant of Old English, in which number and placement of accents is the dominant scheme, and number and placement of unaccented syllables is variable. This will be discussed in some detail later in this chapter.

---

5. *The Rhythmic Structure of Music* (Chicago: University of Chicago Press, 1960).

6. "In addition, the theorists of the last three hundred years have universally understood meter to be a conceptual source of accent interpretation, a context of regularly recurring structural accents and weak beats with which, or against which, freer rhythmic designs may play." Maury Yeston, *The Stratification of Musical Rhythm* (New Haven: Yale University Press, 1976), p. 33.

7. For example, Sheridan Baker, "English Meter *Is* Quantitative," *College English* 21:6 (March 1960), 309–15.

3. Syllabic verse, in which the number of syllables per line is held to a pattern but accents vary in number and placement (poetry by Dylan Thomas, Marianne Moore, Kenneth Rexroth, Alan Stephens, etc.).

4. Accentual–syllabic verse, in which both number of syllables and number and placement of accents are held constant depending on classical structures of foot type and line length.

This last has been the system used for the overwhelming majority of English-language poetry; it is the one we all learn in school. It is also that which would exclusively appear to have provided analogues for the analysis of musical rhythm.

The unit of measure (in all but 3 above) is traditionally the poetic foot. The most viable definition for me is that of T. S. Omond, who sees the metrical line as a series of equal time periods, each of which is usually occupied by syllables and usually characterized by one stressed syllable.[8] Before proceeding, however, we must affirm a vital distinction, that between *meter* and *rhythm*. Simply, these are, respectively, the steady and free pulses. The meter is a fixed and steady abstract (or, as Yeston says [n. 6 *supra*], "conceptual") norm against which the rhythm, the constantly changing acceleration and slowing, syncopation, anticipation, shift of stress, and so on, is counterpointed. When we scan a poem we mark the rhythm, not the meter. The metrical scheme of iambic pentameter has been a favorite of poets writing in English, but the variety that may be achieved rhythmically over that abstract steady pulse may easily be demonstrated.

> *At the round earth's imagin'd corners, blow* (Donne)
> *Fine knacks for ladies, cheap, choice, brave and new* (Dowland)
> *Fair face show friends, when riches do abound* (Googe)
> *And the distortions of ingrown virginity* (Auden)
> *(life to life; breathing to breathing)* (Cummings)
> *Felt the light of her eyes into his life* (Tennyson)
> *Tomorrow and tomorrow and tomorrow* (Shakespeare)
> *Crushed. Why do men then now not reck his rod?* (Hopkins)

The practicability of Omond's definition can be seen easily from the Cummings line—a foot is usually occupied by syllables, but, as in the third foot of the line, this may not necessarily be so. Four lines by Archibald MacLeish will demonstrate this further.

> *Mountain Time: Ocean Time: of the islands:*
> *Of waters after the islands some of them waking*
> *Where noon here is night there: some*
> *Where noon is the first few stars they see or the last one.*

> —THE FALL OF THE CITY

8. *Metrical Rhythm* (reprint Norwood, Pa.: Norwood Editions, 1978).

The foot can also be overloaded, as in some of Hopkins's poetry, but if this is extended too far, secondary accents begin to emerge to be heard as extra primary accents:

> Felix Randal the farrier, O is he dead then? my duty all ended
> Who have watched his mold of man, big-boned and hardy-handsome
> Pining, pining, toll time when reason rambled in it and some
> Fatal four disorders, fleshed there, all contended?

> —FELIX RANDAL

Using the apparatus of traditional scansion, we indicate through this notational shorthand patterns of rhythmic stress and pause.

That part of Omond's definition that creates question grows from realizing that although the metrical foot is isochronous, the rhythmic foot as we hear it, as it actually occurs, is not. No absolute rhythmic evenness of length is ever present; the rhythmic position of stressed syllables may occur earlier or later than that of their metric counterparts (unless one is satisfied to write such lines as "Hurray! hurray! hurray! hurray! hurray!")[9]

In poetry the meter exists unheard. In music the presence of the meter may be constantly in the hearing in such cases as an oom-pah-pah marching band or an Alberti bass, and it is provided in the abstract, heard or not, by the conductor for ensemble pieces. A more immediate example is that of classic jazz, in which the meter, played as background by the rhythm instruments, provides a steady pulse over which the solo instruments work in varying rhythmic shapes. An analogue to this is the use of the steady 2/4 string bass pattern in Stravinsky's *Histoire du soldat* as a background for rhythmically variable lines in the other instruments. At the other extreme, the meter may become simply a "felt beat," perceptible solely to the performers, whether from a conductor or not.[10] The similarity here between the poetic metrical foot and the musical measure is, I trust, obvious.

> For meter to be present, there must be not only periodically recurring pulses but two levels of rhythmic activity, one moving more slowly than another and grouping it into regular units. . . . Yeston concludes logically that a single level cannot possess meter for it cannot move more slowly than itself.[11]

9. Cf. Yvor Winters, *In Defense of Reason* (Denver: University of Denver Press, 1943), pp. 544–5, for a compact discussion of this material.

10. "It is as if the music were painted upon a completely blank surface defined only by a constant pulse. With such a foundation one feels no necessity for constantly reiterating or calling attention to the pulse which is always felt, be it accented or merely implied." Jack Montrose, "Jazz and the Composer," liner notes to *Arranged by Montrose*, World Pacific record PJ-1214. This pulse, heard or unheard, may define the beat equally well on steady 2 and 4 ("fat back") as on 1 and 3.

11. Gary Wittlich, review of Yeston's book, *JMT*, ibid., 357.

The words "logically" and "regular" suggest an evenness perfectly workable in the common practice music with which Yeston and most other scholars are concerned. In the larger view, however, there are some problems raised by this quotation. First, I hope the reader by this time finds obvious that what Wittlich (and Yeston) is actually getting at is that there cannot be *rhythm* without the steady pulse (meter) against which it may operate. As Aaron Copland puts it, "Of course you cannot stay off the beat unless you know where that beat is. Here again freedom is interesting only in relation to regularity."[12]

A second problem may be worked out by the realization that, unlike the poet, the composer may alter or elasticize meter as he may wish, most commonly through changing time signatures. What governs how the performer and listener may pace themselves through such music? I have previously gotten at this[13] with the idea of what I have called pulse, that personal inner rhythm against which each of us paces any passage of time.[14] It is what determines how we handle ritardandi, for example, even in steady meter, or how long we hold a fermata, or how we deal with rubato. This pulse is not only variable among individuals but variable also depending on the occasion, the time of day, our mood, whatever. It is involved with the remark, in James Tenney's anecdote, made to Tenney by Carl Ruggles, that the most difficult counterpoint to write was "one-voice counterpoint." Peter Yates noted "how I watched a young Australian composer tap a strict beat while listening to the final five minutes of *Fontana Mix*, which he was hearing for the first time."[15] It is the means by which we order seemingly unordered sound.

> Rhythmic designs are generally observed to be not simply patterns of pitches of specific durations, but they are also understood to be *interpreted* structures; i.e., they are shaped by the location of accents and weak beats that are created by some aspect of a sound—its duration, intensity, or pitch—in the context of other sounds.[16]

12. *Music and Imagination* (Cambridge: Harvard University Press, 1952), pp. 86–7.

13. Cf. n. 2.

14. Wilson Coker also recognizes this phenomenon: "The unit of temporal measurement is the *pulse*, a regularly recurrent release of energy which is often called a beat. To a listener the pulse of sonorous motion is probably felt more often than conceptualized, for pulse is most often associated with one's acquaintance with the physiological facts of either the stride of walking at normal relaxed paces (i.e., pace = ca. 76–80 m.m.) or the heartbeat when one is engaged in normal activity (i.e., beat = ca. 68–72 m.m.)" *Music and Meaning* (New York: Collier-Macmillan, Ltd., 1972), p. 51. The often-cited statement by Gaforius may perhaps here be reinvoked, that the frequency of the tactus is equivalent to the "pulse beat of a quietly breathing man." (Cited by Gustave Reese, *Music in the Renaissance* (New York: W. W. Norton, 1954), p. 179.)

15. Letter to the author, 9 March 1968.

16. Yeston, pp. 32–3. Not only may we be asked by the conventional barring to apply rhythmic order in a certain fashion, but, lacking such a cue, we may impose an ordering

This problem is of course analogous to its counterpoint in poetry. Syllables have different weight. Accented syllables in particular may vary in weight, with the poet organizing the movement of a line by emphasis of certain accented syllables and down-playing others.[17] Campion, among others, acknowledges this: no "impediment except position . . . can alter the accent of any sillable in our English verse,"[18] pointing out the importance of context. Accent may also be a function of phonetic energy, as musical accent may obtain from intensity of timbre; of underlining; of italics; of the actual stressing a particular syllable with a diacritical mark; even as a function of syntax, of "meaning-accent." Word order within a sentence of poetry can be altered to emphasize or shift rhythmic importance. A standard example is the many possible rearrangements of Gray's line, "The ploughman homeward plods his weary way," from *Elegy Written in a Country Churchyard.*[19]

Poetry has available yet another level of counterpoint, however, that of syntactical or grammatical unit against metrical unit, the sentence against the line.

From Edmund Spenser [probably also from Sidney] in English verse the finest art was employed in running over the verse line so as to build up larger units of movement. . . . This too is more an affect of syntax than anything else; the grammatical unit, the sentence, is draped over the metrical unit, the line, so as to play off the pauses demanded at line-endings (and sometimes within the line) by meter. This is not to "break" the pentameter (or more generally the verse line of whatever length) but rather to submerge it, by incorporating the line into larger and more intricate rhythmical units.[20]

---

rhythm upon what Yeston refers to as "uninterpreted strings" of durational values (pp. 35–36; note his examples p. 36). Christopher Leuba: "Inadvertently, our bodies respond unevenly to the changes between notes, depending upon the *relative* positions of the notes within the pulse, or 'beat.' For instance, we play differently than

"Dexterity," *Woodwind World* 17:3 (May–June 1978), p. 41.

17. The matter becomes considerably more complex with a poet who appears to be controlling movement through variance also of the weight of *un*accented syllables, as Jonson.

18. *Observations in the Art of English Poesie.* A concise approach to contemporary linguists' concern with number and nature of degrees of stress is E. L. Epstein, *Language and Style* (London: Methuen & Co., 1978), p. 45 ff. I prefer, however, to go with Campion and with Winters, in a functional and contextual classification of stress into primary or main stressed or accented syllables, syllables of secondary accent, and syllables of negligible stress. See the Hopkins example cited above.

19. Milton is particularly effective in using this property of arrangement. It is much more easily accomplished, of course, in highly inflectional languages, as Latin.

20. Donald Davie, *Ezra Pound* (New York: Oxford University Press, 1964), p. 44.

The musical equivalent of the grammatical unit is of course the phrase, but since music ordinarily admits no generally accepted convention of grouping metrical units into predetermined and perceptible larger units of constant length, this sort of organization is usually available only through counterpoint. Here of course music has the advantage, since it need not be limited to one voice. An equivalent might be the chaconne/passacaglia structure, or any similarly fixed ostinato, as in some of Lou Harrison's pieces that organize repeating units at various levels of articulation. A fixed pattern of harmonic areas can provide a ''line''-like unit against which the ''sentences'' may be moved; the ''changes'' of jazz qualify here, and a notable example would be Lee Konitz's performance on ''Lover Man,'' (Pacific recording PJLP-2). Perhaps the most challenging examples are in the work of Ralph Shapey, in which fixed metrical-grouping ''line''-units, in themselves working in what is often a complex-appearing contrast of rhythm against meter, can form the basis against which and over which another rhythmic voice (or voices) may be counterpointed. Further, these ''line''-units may be repeated unaltered in the varying environment of what other voices are doing or may slowly metamorphose as the music progresses. *Configuration* (1964), for flute and piano, provides an excellent example. The second movement, cited below beginning at measure 3, uses a steady ostinato figure in the piano, with this note from the composer: ''Pno part to be played in strict metronome tempo. Flute has 16 ♩'s over 4 measures of Pno $\frac{4}{4}$; however no attempt is to be made to keep it together; fl. must be free.'' The particular flute passage ends at the start of bar 12, where the players are instructed, ''bring together.''

EXAMPLE 2.1

Rhythmic Organization:
Contemporary Analogues

So far (I hope) so good, but we have purposely limited ourselves to poetry that is made using the accentual–syllabic structure and to its comparable musical manifestation—common-practice style, metrically oriented
music. The literature generally leaves undiscussed those constructs of
musical rhythm that do not relate to this model; what has been done tries,
with little success, to fit it into the tradition. Nobody, to my knowledge,
has approached the problem in terms of the contemporaneous poetic analogues.

Space here allows only mention of that particular American prosody
that developed on the line of Whitman, Pound, Williams, and Olson; a
readable if contentious treatment of most of it is Edwin Fussell's *Lucifer
in Harness*. This kind of "modern" poetry, generally lumped under the
catch-all term "free verse," appears to many readers to lack any manner
of metrical organization, with the results that, first, any analytic approach
seems unavailable and, second, the assumption is too often made that one
can write such poetry merely by breaking up any chunk of reasonably
"poetic" prose into irregular-length lines and stacking them up in a column. Both assumptions are gross misconceptions.

The foot for free verse, as for its varied successors and offshoots, is
succinctly defined by Winters: "one heavily accented syllable, an unlimited number of unaccented syllables, and an unlimited number of syllables
of secondary accent."[21] It can thus be seen to be properly a variety of
accentual verse. William Carlos Williams's "variable foot"[22] is exactly
this, easily seen by Williams's later practice of setting the three feet of his
line separately on the page.

> *Yellow centers, crimson petals*
> *and the reverse,*
> *dandelion, love-in-a-mist*
> *corn flowers,*
> *thistle and others*
> *the names and perfumes I do not know.*
> *The woods are filled with holly*
> *(I have told you, this*

21. *In Defense of Reason*, p. 112. The whole of Winters' section "The Scansion of Free
Verse" is of vital importance, particularly his demonstrations with such poems as Wallace
Stevens' "The Snow Man".
22. Williams's own words on the variable foot, with examples he provides, are handily
presented by John Malcolm Brinnin, *William Carlos Williams* (Minneapolis: University of
Minnesota Press, 1963), pp. 32–4, and, less extensively, elsewhere.

> *is a fiction, pay attention),*
> > *the yellow flag of the French fields is here*
> > *and a congeries of other flowers*
> *as well: daffodils*
> > *and gentian, the daisy, columbine*
> > > *petals*
> *myrtle, dark and light*
> > *and calendulas.*

—from *Paterson*, book V

And of course Omond's definition applies here as well as with earlier poetry, the difference being perhaps that the free-verse foot, the variable foot, occupies more time than the accentual–syllabic foot or the quantitative foot. The next step after Williams, projective verse, developed by Charles Olson and the other so-called "Black Mountain" poets, includes immediate concern with breath units as an added prosodic criterion of measure.[23] "Ideally," says Allen Ginsberg, "each line of *Howl* is a single breath unit."[24] The development of linguistic scholarship has furnished new information on the phenomena of speech, and poets have not been behindhand in availing themselves of this.[25] The reader should notice that these current directions are thoroughly concerned with poetry as growing from and presenting speech rhythm and, in addition, with the means of notation of audible speech on the page.

23. This is, after all, no novelty. Initially the classical theory of properly proportioned *membra* and definition of *commata* and *cola* in rhetorical prose took into account the limitations of the human voice at speaking pitch. Morris Croll has this to say ("The Cadence of English Oratorical Prose," *Studies in Philology* XVI (January 1919), 23): "A member is followed by a rest, or a pause, which is a breathing interval, and it very rarely exceeds twenty syllables in length, because the heightened energy of utterance required in public speaking cannot be maintained for a greater number of syllables than this without an opportunity fully to recover the breath." Gascoigne imputed the caesura to musicians (*Elizabethan Critical Essays*, ed. Gregory Smith (Oxford: Oxford University Press, 1904, I, 54)); Campion remarks that "our English monasillables enforce many breathings." (*Observations. . . .*)

24. "Notes Written on Finally Recording *Howl*," liner notes to Fantasy Records 7006 (1959). Those wishing to follow these directions are urged to consult the synoptic *The Poetics of the New American Poetry*, ed. Donald M. Allen and Warren Tallman (New York: Grove Press, 1973).

25. The following illuminating passage by Lionel Kearns appears in a work of such ephemeral nature that it may not easily be found; I therefore provide it here despite its length.

There is one important type of English speech rhythm in particular which suffers in most page transcriptions of poems, and that is stress-rhythm. The linguists tell us that our syllables, that each of these clusters (called a phonemic clause) contains one syllable which takes a heavy stress (called a primary stress in a four degree system) and ends in a terminal juncture (that break in articulation which is sometimes signalled on

It is the advantage of the typewriter that, due to its rigidity and its space precisions, it can, for a poet, indicate exactly the breath, the pauses, the suspensions even of syllables, the juxtapositions even of parts of phrases, which he intends. For the first time he can, without the convention of rhyme and meter, record the listening he has done to his own speech and by that one act indicate how he would want any reader, silently or otherwise, to voice his work.[26]

Writing about musical rhythm that includes late twentieth-century material has been slight compared with the scholarship in music of earlier periods, although Gary Wittlich's chapter in *Aspects of 20th Century Music* is a plausible start, as are articles by Erickson and Smither.[27] The crux of the matter is recognizable in these articles. Both Smither and Erickson, the latter despite his expressed interest in "turning away from the hierarchical rhythmic relationships toward a rhythm of constantly emerging and changing patterns of relationship," discuss music in which these hierarchies are present.[28] Despite elasticity of meter and complexity of rhythmic gesture, such works as Boulez's *Le marteau sans maître,* Stockhausen's *Zeitmasse,* Carter's second string quartet, and the like work from the established and organized relationships between two (and sometimes more) levels of musical movement related hierarchically. This is also the case with compositions that may dispense entirely with a no-

the page by a punctuation mark and sometimes not signalled at all), and that in sustained utterance the amount of time between two primary stresses tends to be the same irrespective of the amount of material between them (this last linguistic phenomenon being called isochronism). It follows that the stress-rhythm of a particular utterance will depend on the character and arrangement of its phonemic clauses. And if the poet is going to make formal use of this type of speech rhythm in his works he will regard the phonemic clause as his basic structural unit of sound.

(Introduction to *Songs of Circum/stance* (Vancouver: Private printing, 1962).) The overlap of formal linguistics into music has largely been on a basis of the application of large-order systems and theories, posited for language, to music, with what seem to me constrictive and erroneous results (cf. Eugene Narmour, *Beyond Schenkerism* (Chicago: University of Chicago Press, 1977), ch. 9, for an illuminating discussion of this). On the other hand, use of specific phenomena of linguistics to deal with the nature of musical immediacies can provide, I believe, useful apparatus, as Alexandra Pierce, "Juncture," *ITO* 3:6 (September 1977), pp. 23–34.

26. Charles Olson, "Projective Verse," *The Poetics* . . ., p. 154. Cf. my previously cited article (n. 2) for further discussion of notation in contemporary poetry.

27. *Aspects of 20th Century Music* (Englewood Cliffs, N.J.: Prentice Hall, 1975); Robert Erickson, "Time-Relations," *JMT* 7:2 (Winter 1963), 174–93; Howard Smither, "The Rhythmic Analysis of 20th-Century Music," *JMT* 8:1 (Spring 1964), 55–88. The latter is mal-cited as "Smithers" by Yeston (p. 27).

28. Possibilities of perception and organization of hierarchies are discussed by Thomas Fay, "Perceived Hierarchic Structure in Language and Music," *JMT* 15: 1 and 2 (1971), pp. 112–37.

tated metric scheme and indicate time's passage by marking every so many seconds to provide performer pacing rate through the score, as say Elliott Schwartz's *Septet,* Berio's flute *Sequenza,* Earle Brown's *Hodograph I,* or Richmond Browne's *Reri Velocitatem.*[29]

The crossover point occurs when any kind of metrical basis for the music ceases to exist.[30] Once the governance of such a basis is gone, the pacing often depends on the individual performer's relationship to personal pulse. This pulse may of course be controlled against what the performer is hearing from other players or other sound sources, metrical or otherwise. In Morton Feldman's *Piece for Four Pianos* (1957), each player's progress through the similar musical material is governed by his own sense of "rightness" as to when each particular event should occur.

A number of other challenging approaches are reflected in works composed in the early 1960s. Larry Austin, in *Continuum* (1964), establishes two kinds of relationships in time. The first is for each player, who is given notes of relative-only durations (long and short) that he plays and groups against his own pacing; the second links various players in two and three and, on occasion, the tutti, by vertical dotted-line cues on the score, providing an over-structure of ear-matched "rendezvous points" that furnish an inner self-measuring and self-generating order that is only superfluously metrical, if at all, since it is a result of the adaptation of each player's movement against pulse to arrive at the specific score points at the proper time. Austin was working at this date with what he termed "open style": "through-composed motion pieces with rude, violent gestures dominating."[31] An operative word here might be "gestures," since both in recent music and recent poetry this is of extensive concern.[32] The adapted accentual foot, be it termed variable, projective, or otherwise,

29. Originally works in what has come to be referred to as spatial notation (as say Cage's *Music of Changes* (1951) and some of Earle Brown's pieces in *Folio* (1952–3)) use the time = notational space guide for the "steady pulse" of the meter. The later *Folio* works break with this. Cf. Sydney Hodkinson's paper in *Proc. ASUC* 5 (1970) on rhythmic and conducting problems of music in "conventional 'closed-form' non-graphic notation."

30. "First, there is the kind of composition that appears to exhibit absolutely no regularity of motion on any level. This can be caused by either of two conditions: The music is exactly what it appears to be in that there is nothing in it resembling a pulse; or the music is so saturated with conflicting rates of regular motion that it is purposeless to begin to specify any of them, since they obscure each other utterly." Yeston, p. 149.

31. Larry Austin, notes to Advance Recordings FGR-10S (1969).

32. Although Europeans were working with some of the same ideas at this time, the musical units were inevitably related to metrical and other structural hierarchies. Stockhausen, for example, defines moment–form: "Each moment whether a state or a process, is individual and self-regulated, and able to sustain an independent existence." (Cited by Karl H. Worner, *Stockhausen: Life and Work* (London: Faber, 1973), p. 46.) A typical explanation of the importance of interdependent nesting structures is ibid., pp. 95–6, as well as an idea of musical gesture: "the more a group becomes concentrated—in other words the fewer the

with its expanded room to move, its more relaxed overall motion, its dominance by breath energy and speech energy (cf. Olson), its emphasis on the audible, and its employment in "through-composed" fashion— "Form is never more than an extension of content" (Robert Creeley)— serves as close analogue for many present-day composers' rhythmic practice, whether or not working over a meter.

Harold Budd, in the series of *New Work* pieces (1967–1972, each of the six for different wind instrument and piano, the same piano part being used for all), works with two simultaneous player-paced musical time lines with the sense that each player, independently, occupies and is qualifying his own individual time and space. Each part, which may begin anywhere (and is played through until that beginning point has been reached), is notated as a number of boxes, most containing musical events, from one note to many, although some are empty, and these boxes are to be regarded as isochronous, with the event(s) placed whenever the performer may wish during the time of the box. The relationship to the Omond (Winters, Williams, etc.) poetic foot is immediate. There is, obviously, no time-signatured or audible meter.

The concern with the poem as a field, affirmed by Williams and Olson (q.v.), has one obvious analogue in considering the notated musical page as a field. Early work in this direction provided written musical units that were chosen, by random means or player preference, for consecutive performance.[33]

Another step away from the original accentual-syllabic meter/rhythm

---

elements it conjoins in a simple order and the less repetitions it contains—the more it approaches the state of a unique and unrepeatable shape" p. 96.

The American tradition is noted by Eric Salzman beginning as early as Ives: "He wanted a speaking kind of music, a music that could be jotted down to convey fresh impressions and thoughts, that could flow with the naturalness of plain speech; a music that could somehow get across that impenetrable barrier between art and life, not to 'express' nature but to flow along as part of it." (*Twentieth-Century Music: An Introduction* (Englewood Cliffs, N.J.: Prentice-Hall, 1967), p. 131.) An interesting early approach to a speech-rhythm basis for music is in the work of Dane Rudhyar. "While most classical European music, except that of a religious type, is based on the rhythm of the dance, a simple, marked and strictly physical rhythm (even in its most cosmic expression), this music finds its rhythmic source in *Speech*. It is a series of instrumental utterances, having a psycho-physiological and spiritual meaning, but not an intellectual or anecdotic one. It must therefore be played with the freedom and peculiar rhythm of speech, a complex, emotional, metaphysical rhythm. This means that the tyranny of the bar must go." (Introductory notes to *Moments* [Boston: C. C. Birchard & Co., 1930], the works later to be republished as three of the four *Pentagrams*.)

33. One finds reference to Stockhausen's *Klavierstuck* XI (1956) as being the original work in this area, but Earle Brown had thoroughly explored the possibilities of the page as field and so-called "mobile form" with the later works in *Folio*, notably *December 1952*. Sometimes the score controls performer motion in space as well as in time (say Cardew's *Memories of You* (1964).

approach comes with the addition of silence as a contributing, even structural, element, metrically governed or otherwise. The most familiar example to me is my own *Interbalances IV* (1961), for trumpet and reader, in which each performer chooses at any moment from a considerable set of options but is also asked to make silence a part of his own musical construct by allowing it to accrue to gather between the sounded alternatives. There is never any fixed order. The sense of pulse in determining when one performs any alternative, and often which choice he will make, should furnish a constant sense of personal immediacy and involvement to the performer: "The music is not thought of as an "accompaniment" to the narration, nor the narration to the music: work it out that each is a separately developing continuum of sound and silence."[34] Again, large parts of a composition may be silence, whether or not this is measured metrically. In recent work of Lawrence Kucharz the written constant meter is essentially inaudible because of first, the high percentage of the piece being silent and second, the appearance of sound in repeated chords that occur each time at a different steady temporal frequency, with following silence such that this apparent meter tends to shift and blur.[35]

In a number of works beginning ca. 1957, by Christian Wolff, rhythmic articulation is accomplished in several varying fashions, ranging in detail from immediate succession of events interacting among the players (an analogue in ensemble response to "as fast as possible") to waiting, sustaining either sound or silence, until a specified number of other events has been heard or a specified time duration has been counted out. Here again there is a sense of the ongoing musical gestures, both for the ensemble and for the individual player, coalescing and affirming themselves through a variety of possible situations never the same twice.

Mid-twentieth century composers have developed compositional practices involving the organization of musical structure through codification and operation of various "parameters".[36] Relationships are established and developed not merely with such immediately perceptible musical criteria as pitch, duration, density, articulation, and the like, but also with

34. Tritone Press.

35. Further discussion of problems of musical time can be found in Barney Childs, "Music and Time: A Composer's View," *PNM* 15:2 (Spring-Summer 1977), 194–219, and in a number of essays by Jonathan Kramer, most recently "Moment Form in Twentieth Century Music," *MQ* 64:4 (April 1978), pp. 117–194, and "Varieties of Time in Twentieth Century Music," unpublished paper, 1978.

36. "any distinctive attribute of sound in terms of which one sound may be perceived as different from another, or a sound may be perceived to change in time." James Tenney, "META Meta + Hodos," *Journal of Experimental Aesthetics,* 1:1 (1977), p. 4. Some investigation of this rather overworked term is interestingly carried out by Claire Boge, " 'Parameter' in Music and Musical Analysis," *ITO* 3:4 (July 1977), 14–26.

more conceptual gamuts and levels of ordering. For example, a composition might have been written based formally on the following classes of rhythmic organization: (*a*) solo improvisation; (*b*) group improvisation, with a resulting complex and spontaneous performer-interactive rhythmic counterpoint dependent on each player's sense of pulse modified to varying degrees in response to what else may be heard; (*c*) choice of given alternatives performed in choice-determined order, for a soloist, with the result depending upon rhythmic openness or regularity limited by the nature, and number, of rhythmic organizations provided, this in turn implying or affirming metrical organization; (*d*) simultaneous interaction of rhythm by several players' doing (*c*); (*e*) solo material traditionally related to a metrical organization, heard or implied; (*f*) group material thus related to a single metrical base; related "time streams"; (*g*) group material ordered on any scale of compositional rigor by multiply-related or interrelated metrical bases with the possibility that any of these can happen simultaneously and can be controlled by interperformer response to what is being heard. A direction already explored by Ben Johnston in such categorizing of levels of musical variables is that suggested in the following:

> S. S. Stevens presents four kinds of scales of measurement: nominal, ordinal, interval, and ratio. A nominal scale is a collection of equivalent and interchangeable items. An ordinal scale is a collection which is rank-ordered in terms of some attribute. An interval scale is a rank-ordered collection in which the intervals of difference between items are equal. A ratio scale is a rank-ordered collection in which items are related by equal ratios.[37]

Yeston's chapter "Structures from the Interaction of Strata" can serve as a springboard to the more open sorts of interrelationship that Johnston is working with, as well as others. Yeston's idea of "metrical dissonance" is certainly anticipated by Henry Cowell as early as 1919:

> the possibility of joining what might be called metric melody with material metrically harmonic. This may be done by relating the successive metrical

---

37. "Scalar Order as a Compositional Resource," *PNM* 2:2 (Spring-Summer 1964), p. 56 ff. These classifications are developed into a means of dealing with styles of notation by William Duckworth and Edward Brown, *Theoretical Foundations of Music* (Belmont, California: Wadsworth, 1978), ch. 24 ff. An article by Charles Molesworth offers a valuable guide to some poetic stances parallel in nature to directions in recent music. "Gradually this dominant sense of a poem as an autotelic, self-explaining statement, or 'object,' began to lose its force. In its place in the late fifties and early sixties came at least three other metaphoric images for the poem: 1) the poem as a force-field; 2) the poem as a 'leaping' or associatively linked cluster of non-discursive images; and 3) the poem as commentary on some unspoken myth what Galway Kinnell has called a 'palimpsest.' " ("Contemporary Poetry and the Metaphors for the Poem," *The Georgia Review* XXXII:2 (Summer 1978), p. 321.)

units (corresponding to tones) of one part according to the principle of counterpoint, while the units of the simultaneous parts are selected and grouped according to the principle of harmony.[38]

Such complex metrical relationships as those in Cowell's examples and those possible through use of Elliott Carter's metric modulation[39] may be made even more intricate, as those present in certain works by Conlon Nancarrow[40] and potentially accessible in works composed on tape with electronic equipment and by computer. Larger-order organization (macrostructuring) using ratio scale-related time units, dealt with should one wish as the equivalent of the poetic stanza—as that prechance work of John Cage based on time blocks of related lengths[41] and the current enthusiasm for the use of the Fibonacci series and other macrostructural principles—may also be approached by extrapolation from traditional hierarchy-oriented rhythmic analytics. I hope that this chapter so far has demonstrated that by a knowledge of contemporary postaccentual poetic metrics one may also be able to deal with musical work that would appear, using only accentual-syallabic analogues, otherwise incoherent.

Rhythm and "Value"

Any manner or organization, rhythmic or otherwise, may be interpreted from, and imposed upon, a piece of music in whatever fashion one may find satisfactory, and for whatever purpose,[42] and this leads to some commentary in two additional areas of speculation. One of the directions favored by present investigation tends increasingly to isolate the score, or the poem, as a separate and pristine construct.

> This goes to the heart of my quarrel with the stylisticians: in their rush to establish an inventory of fixed significances, they bypass the activity in the course of which significances are, if only momentarily, fixed. I have said be-

38. *New Musical Resources* (reprint New York: Something Else Press, 1969), p. 77. Cowell's pioneering work with the interaction of harmonic and rhythmic proportions has been inexplicably overlooked by present-day scholars.

39. Cf. particularly "The Time Dimension in Music" and "Music and the Time Screen," both now available in *The Writings of Elliott Carter* (Bloomington: University of Indiana Press, 1977).

40. Also overlooked; work not printed until 1973 (*Study #21* in *Soundings* 7–8 (July–October 1973), pp. 125–47.)

41. Cf. Michael Nyman, *Experimental Music* (London: Studio Vista, 1974) for illuminating discussion on some immediately contemporary approaches to time organization.

42. Cf. David Behrman, "What Indeterminate Notation Determines," *PNM* 3:2 (Spring–Summer 1965), pp. 58–73.

fore that their procedures are arbitrary, and that they acknowledge no constraint on their interpretations of the data. The shape of the reader's [hearer's] experience is the constraint they decline to acknowledge. Were they to make that shape the focus of their analyses, it would lead them to the value conferred by its events. Instead they proceed in accordance with the rule laid down by Martin Joos: "Text signals its own structure," treating the deposit of an activity as if it were the activity itself, as if meanings arose independently of human transactions. As a result, they are left with patterns and statistics that have been cut off from their animating source, banks of data that are unattached to anything but their own formal categories, and are therefore, quite literally, meaningless.[43]

With today's apparent fondness for clearly defined and opposed binary options, the other side of the coin is too often restricted to orientation in psychological terms, the sort of thing described by Yeston as

any theory of perception that attempts to explain how rhythmic organization originates, psychologically or psycho-physiologically, in the human organism and how the organism perceives and responds to organized motion.
A gestalt-oriented approach seeks to uncover the intrinsic operations or constructions of a perception, such as the presumably innate, human tendency to group a series of steady pulses into recurrent cells of two or three pulses each.[44]

Wittlich's review notes Yeston's apparent wish to avoid (perhaps distaste for) this approach, suggesting (in agreement with Fish) that, whereas "Yeston disclaims any intention to produce a theory of human perceptions as a concommitant [sic] of his rhythmic stratification theory (p. 37), the theory ought not to contradict one's experience."[45]

I have recently suggested elsewhere[46] that a new set of assumptions regarding the nature and function of art, one moving largely cross-grained to that we have inherited from the Western European intellectual and cultural tradition, is becoming increasingly available. Both recent music and recent poetry affirm these assumptions and draw upon them. Although complete exposition of this is impossible here, a comment or two about it is necessary. Organization in art has moved from the Renaissance systems and hierarchies, Ramistic classification and logical constructs, concern with perspective and framing, bounding and closed ordering, into a stance from which the perceiver is the source of order and organization

43. Stanley E. Fish, "What is Stylistics?", *Approaches to Poetics*, ed. Seymour Chatman (New York: Columbia University Press, 1973), p. 131.
44. Yeston, p. 27.
45. Ibid., p. 368.
46. "Time and Music," cf. n. 33, also article on musical continuity, *Proc. ASUC* 6 (1971), pp. 55–64.

and structures can be open and self-generating. Such non-Western world views as those of the so-called "primitive" peoples have become accessible to us as well. R. Murray Schafer illustrates this, in a discussion of non-perspective-oriented societies.

The Eskimos, as Edmund Carpenter has shown, would often continue a drawing over the edge of the drawing surface onto the back of the material, considering it part of the same surface. Carpenter writes:

I know of no example of an Aivilik describing space primarily in visual terms. They don't regard space as static and therefore measurable; hence they have no formal units of spatial measurement, just as they have no uniform divisions of time. The carver is indifferent to the demands of the optical eye; he lets each piece fill its own space, create its own space, create its own world without reference to background or anything external to it. . . . Like sound, each carving creates its own space, its own identity; it imposes its own assumptions.

Carpenter feels the Eskimo's space awareness is acoustic.

Auditory space has no favored focus. It's a sphere without fixed boundaries, space made by the thing itself, not space containing the thing.[47]

An immediate poetical analogue is in the poetry of Wallace Stevens: "Ideas of Order at Key West," for example, or the jar of "Parable of the Jar" which, when placed on the hill in Tennessee, reorders and rebalances everything around it. A good-sized passage from Charles Olson seems important enough to me here to warrant citation in its entirety.

All that comparison ever does is set up a series of reference points: to compare is to take one thing and try to understand it by marking its similarities to or differences from another thing. Right here is the trouble, that each thing is not so much like or different from another thing (these likenesses and differences are apparent) but that such an analysis only accomplishes a *description*, does not come to grips with what really matters: that a thing, any thing, impinges on us by a more important fact, its self-existence, without reference to any other thing, in short, the very character of it which calls our attention to it, which wants us to know more about it, its particularity. This is what we are confronted by, not the thing's "class," any hierarchy, of quality or quantity, but the thing itself, and its *relevance* to ourselves who are the experience of it (whatever it may mean to someone else, or whatever other relations it may have).

47. *The Tuning of the World* (Toronto: McClelland & Stewart, 1977), pp. 157–8. Schafer's book is of signal importance. Cf. also *Technicians of the Sacred*, ed. Jerome Rothenberg (New York: Doubleday, 1969). "unity is achieved—in general by the imposition of some constant or 'key' against which all disparate materials can be measured. A sound, a rhythm, a name, an image, a dream, a gesture, a picture, an action, a silence: any or all of these can function as 'keys.' Beyond that there's no need for consistency, for fixed or discrete meanings. An object is whatever it becomes under the influence of the situation at hand" (p. xxi).

There must be a means of expression for this, a way which is not divisive as all the tag ends and upendings of the Greek way are. There must be a way which bears *in* instead of away, which meets head on what goes on each split second, a way which does not—in order to define—prevent, deter, distract, and so cease the act of, discovering.[48]

It is possible now, in discussing not only the music and poetry but also the means of dealing with them, to have the tools to do the job from a stance which first may draw upon both the psychology-based criticism and the text/analysis approach, and, second, may proceed from the observer-centered and experience-centered position that the previously discussed premises imply.

Fish's phrase "the value conferred by its events" suggests a second concern, one much dealt with by those involved with poetry but perhaps not so much today by the music scholar. Yeston also touches upon this matter:

the unclear relationship of pitch interpretation to rhythm interpretation. The criteria of significance of musical events are clouded by the aforementioned, circular analytic tendency to value a pitch in terms of its accentual placement (rhythm to pitch) while, at the same time, positing an accentual scheme on the basis of pitch value (pitch-to-rhythm).[49]

The words *value* and *significance* are the concern here. Speculation about these is usually part of musical esthetics, and involving rhythm it may range from investigation of the nature imputed by Greek writers to the rhythmic modes to discussion of music in terms of its suitability for assistance in psychotherapy. This general direction, however, has been far more immediately explored in considering poetry, with consistent attention upon the contribution of prosody to the esthetic functioning of the poem. A current statement of position on moral effect is John Gardner's *On Moral Fiction*.[50] Although Mr. Gardner's involvement is largely, as

---

48. "Human Universe," *The Poetics* . . ., pp. 164–5. The kind of persisting confusion which may be removed by an understanding of the acoustic space/visual space differences is suggested by Mary Ann Caws's remarks about the poetry of René Char: "We have opted for a *spatial* conception as opposed to the more temporal one which would be that of a musical composition," and, in a footnote, "René Char is clearly closer to the world of painters than to that of musicians, the spatial vision imposing its particular character even on the moral conception. There is here, as always, another point of view. . . . Roger Laporte says the opposite 'cette dimension temporelle plus importante que la spatiale.'" *The Presence of René Char* (Princeton: Princeton University Press, 1976), p. 9.

49. Yeston, p. 33.

50. (New York: Basic Books, 1978).

his title suggests, with fiction, he also deals in passing with the other arts. The contemporary reader may feel that this kind of speculation concerning music went out with John Sullivan Dwight, for whom music and the other arts should "remedy the defects of a materialistic society by 'familiarizing men with the beautiful and infinite',"[51] and Gardner does from time to time hold forth in this vein, but the matter is not that easily dismissed.

> The morality of music is faithfulness to the immutable laws of musical gravity (the laws by which melody tends to fall and progressions sink to resolution and rest) and faithfulness to the particular work's emotional energy. . . .
> Obviously, feeling can come from texture or from structure . . . but structure also carries feeling, as we see beyond doubt when we follow a progression of musical events or, still more baldly, when a familiar melody comes back. And in music as elsewhere, structure, not texture, is primary, though it cannot stand alone.[52]

This is obviously a real hot potato, and I have neither space nor inclination to spend much time on it here, choosing instead to suggest some possible approaches by once again drawing on poetic considerations in an effort to illuminate musical ones. If a work of art *is* held to convey moral value, whatever we may decide this to be, the artist's generated structure, or order, and our ability to perceive this and to impose and interpret it as we may wish—perhaps beyond this order—will inevitably be involved. What part of this can rhythm have? All else being equal, it is possible through rhythmic ordering to affirm this value?

I. A. Richards invents an interesting experiment in this connection. The question he is discussing is that concerning first, necessary conformity of poetry to metrical patterns and, second, "the notion that poetic rhythm is independent of sense."[53]

> It is easy, however, to show how much the rhythm we *ascribe* to words (and even their inherent rhythm as sounds) is influenced by our apprehension of their meanings. . . . If the meaning of the words is irrelevant to the form of the verse, and if this independent form possesses aesthetic virtue . . . it should be possible to take some recognized masterpiece of poetic rhythm and compose, with nonsense syllables, a double or dummy which at least comes recognizably near to possessing the same virtue.

51. H. Wiley Hitchcock, *Music in the United States* (Englewood Cliffs, N. J.: Prentice Hall, 1974), p. 55.

52. Gardner, pp. 62–3.

53. *Practical Criticism* (reprint New York: Harcourt, Brace, n.d.) The material cited is from pp. 220–1.

His "dummy" is entertainingly based on Milton's *On the Morning of Christ's Nativity*. He then continues:

> But the illustration will also support a subtler argument against anyone who affirms that the mere sound of verse has *independently* any considerable aesthetic virtue. For he will *either* have to say that this verse is valuable . . . *or* he will have to say that it is the differences in *sound* between this purified dummy and the original which deprive the dummy of poetic merit. In which case he will have to account for the curious fact that just those transformations which redeem it as sound, should also give it the sense and feeling we find in Milton. A staggering coincidence, unless the meaning were highly relevant to the effect of the form.

So far, then, we are thrown back in music to having to deal with the "content" (i.e. pitch) and rhythm problem. "Such arguments, . . ." Richards continues, ". . . do not tend to diminish the power of the sound (the inherent rhythm) when it works *in conjunction with sense and feeling.*" Of course the reader will have realized immediately that the analogy cannot be transferred directly from poetry to music, since the "sense" of music does not depend on that signifying convention operative within language so that the noise made by a word stands for something other than itself. A work which is agreeably close to the premise of Richards's experiment is of course John Cage's *Cheap Imitation*, which can be considered in this direction. Reginald Smith Brindle's distinction between "classical" and "serial" music is also of interest here.

> *In classical music the rhythmic patterns remain constant. Diversity is achieved by using different notes:*
>
> [the opening of Beethoven's 5th Symphony cited]
>
> Here it is the rhythms which give complete identity to the music, while the actual notes used contribute considerably less to the music's uniqueness.
> *In serial music it is the notes which remain the same (i.e. the series). Diversity is achieved by using different rhythms.*
> In serial music, it is the series which gives identity and unity to the music. Rhythmic configuration cannot do so, as it is always changing.[54]

Smith Brindle includes in this section a number of citations from serial works with the pitches altered to fit tonal models, and from traditional works with the pitches altered by substituting sets.

One of the most dedicated proponents of the moral effects of poetry and of how it relates to the machinery of a poem is Yvor Winters. He asserts[55]

---

54. *Serial Composition* (London: Oxford University Press, 1966), p. 33.

55. *In Defense of Reason.* The interested reader is urged to read carefully Winters's chapter "Preliminary Problems" in its entirety. Winters is, curiously, all but overlooked by Gardner, whose case Winters's work would have provided powerful apparatus to affirm.

that a poem, differing from prose by being written in verse (or, in the terms of this article, in metrical language) is such that "The rhythm of verse permits the expression of more powerful feeling than is possible in prose when such feeling is needed, and it permits at all times the expression of finer shades of feeling." Each word, he continues, "has a conceptual content, however slight; each word, exclusive, perhaps, of the particles, communicates vague associations of feeling." We may well have also these "vague associations" from music, depending upon our familiarity with its particular conventions, which we will have gained from our acculturation; the Rothenberg passage cited above (fn. 45) suggests how any audible feature may so function, and the usual phrase in our culture for unfamiliar music is, "It doesn't *mean* anything." Musical rhythm is, I would therefore assume, involved in some fashion with a response growing from some level of "feeling." Stuart Jay Petock states this position precisely.

> I believe that value is proportional to the possibility of engaging in an activity in which one structures the material the work of art presents to consciousness within one's own experience. I hold that the excitement of that activity is precisely why we like the arts, and that the more intense that activity is—the more we have to do in order to know the work of art as coherent structure—the more exciting the art will be and the more we will value it.[56]

Is "coherent structure" by itself, that there for us to discover or that we impose, sufficient? Gardner, as we have seen, thinks not: "Some of our new music is cold-blooded, theoretical, following the directions worked out by Boulez and Babbett [*sic*]."[57] "Contrivance," says Petock, "is often the failure of taste,"[58] and "so far as the creative process is performed according to a plan, the structure of the process itself will be adherent, even, I should think, if the plan from which the process was determined was creation within a coherent process."[59] On the one hand, then, we have suggestions that some manner of "spontaneity" or "inspiration" is required for esthetic validity in opposition to "contrivance" or too much emphasis on the "theoretical" (Petock's "coherent" and "adherent"); on the other hand, we may place the view that artistic validity is directly proportional in some fashion to the degree of apparent "control" demonstrated by the artist. And this "control," the results of the artist's exercising some sort of "responsibility," may of course be revealed

56. "Expression in Art: The Feelingful Side of Aesthetic Experience," *The Journal of Aesthetics and Art Criticism,* XXX:3 (Spring 1972), 302.

57. Gardner, p. 64.

58. Petock, 308.

59. Ibid., 306.

through the application of analytic machinery which can itself become equated to compositional validity in the accuracy of its own process.[60]

One's position on the nature and necessity of the function of rhythm toward rational and moral ends, and on the degree and importance of this function as a criterion of "value," depends therefore upon toward which of these apparent poles one may incline. What A may regard as hopelessly mechanistic and soulless contrivance and gimmickry, B may feel to be that unique organic process by which the music is animated and takes its nature and through which it operates. C may hold jazz to be corrupting, immoral, and socially destructive; D may feel it to be a source of transcendent musical inspiration and expression. Within the communicative boundaries of poetry (Richards) or the language-like qualities of music (Gardner), what seems to fit what we choose to regard as moral will take place; the music and the poetry will be assumed to be *about* something, and our acculturated conventions will decide how we respond not only to the sounds made but also what the *about*-ness is. The sound, as Pope writes, will seem an echo to the sense.

We seem to have inherited belief that the presence of, and primacy of, structure (or "form") is a necessary concomitant to any kind of communicative validity.[61] If communication theory is accepted, then this becomes further explicable. Assuming a common convention between originator and receiver, the more detailing of the decisions made in encoding the message (with the corresponding reduction of entropy), the more "information" can be communicated. This is easily expanded to assume that, through acculturated convention, certain structures are properly used to a communicative end only when dealing with certain material. What makes a funeral march? Why isn't Spenserian stanza suitable for a translation of *Beowulf?*[62]

By this time I hope that it is evident that in spoken language the rhythm comes gratuitously along with the sound. Any passage will have unique patternings of stress depending on the words chosen by the speaker's ongoing direction of communication, whether or not he has paid attention to organizing these patternings. Aside from order we may choose to impose, we do not isolate pitch and rhythm; we are too busy listening to what is "meant." To reinvoke Creeley, we may say that form is solely an extension of content. And as Richards demonstrates, without the signifying "content" stress patterns appear arbitrary and developed simply in terms

60. I have discussed this to some degree in the paper on musical continuity, cf. n. 45.
61. Cf. Kenneth Burke's discussion of what he refers to as "conventional form" in *Counter-Statement* (Berkeley: University of California Press, 1968), p. 124 ff.
62. For a challenging example, consider the fugue movement of Rochberg's fourth string quartet and the composer's comments on the work.

of sound for its own sake, as when we hear a speaker in a language unknown to us. We can still be concerned with the extension of heard instants, with the sentence or the utterance or the phrase or whatever, but without the ''sense'' to follow, rhythmic values (as well as others such as pitch and timbre and density) take on an existence for the listener as independently organizing entities to the attention, an existence quite different from that subordinate and interwoven function they serve when we are following what's being ''meant''—that is, we begin to listen to the sound as ''music.''

A unique example is Alvin Lucier's ''I Am Sitting in a Room.''[63] A passage of spoken language is, by consecutive rerecording on tape with an air mike, gradually transformed into a pattern of pitches, these dependent on the resonant frequencies of the particular room being used, organized by the rhythm of this spoken passage. Both rhythms and pitches increasingly occupy our listening attention, emerging in our hearing as independent structures. Pitch shapes and rhythmic articulations tend to replace the ''signifying'' nature of audible language and, depending on the hearer's acculturation systems, may also replace the ''what it's about.'' The convention of the adaptability of music to serve as background for eye art in this fashion needs only a single illustration here: Composer Philip Winsor and film maker Tom Palazzolo, showing five of Palazzolo's films each in turn accompanied by the same tape composition by Winsor, found that the music seemed to fit the film superbly in every case.

As long, therefore, as music seems to a listener to be ''about'' something, through its similarities to audible ''signifying'' language—its time-extended nature, apparent movement, speechlike complexes of pitches and inflections and rhythms—he will deal with it in whatever his acculturated responses furnish him as a basis for being ''about,'' and order and organization and structure will be sought for as part of this end, with judgments about moral or esthetic value following, these latter being inescapably interwrought (as Petock and others explain) with his feelings. In the esthetic abstract, no work can originally be ''bad'': presumably the poet or composer has chosen whatever is in the poem or composition because for him at the moment of choice it seemed, consciously or spontaneously, the best choice available. Even if the artist has set out purposely to write a ''bad'' work (who, after all, can know this without some sort of admission by the artist?), he has very likely done so as well as he can; he has still

---

63. *Source* 7 (1970), p. 60, and the following included recording. Another interesting case is music whose rhythm is directly based on the movement of a specific passage of language, as on occasion with Hindemith (the last movement of the alto horn sonata, the recitative movement of the sonata for two pianos).

made what seem to him the "right" choices, has selected the material that seems to him best to work as "bad."

In summary, an investigation of the directions taken by rhythm and meter in recent poetry can furnish a valuable alternative position in dealing with recent musical rhythmic practice, circumventing that apparent dead end regretted by most of those to whom interrelating hierarchic structure serves as a sole resource. Even more pervasively useful, however, can be that particular acoustic-centered, inside-out thinking I have suggested in my discussion of Schafer and the poetry of Wallace Stevens as well as the citations from Olson;[64] its adaptability and that very lack of insistence on "logic" and rigor that may repel those settled in our traditionally accultured stances would suggest that through extended development and application an entire range of new thinking about music may be opened.

---

64. And outlined briefly in "Music and Time," cf. n. 35.

3

Carlton Gamer

ET SETERA: SOME TEMPERAMENTAL SPECULATIONS

Introduction

For the past several years I have engaged in that most speculative of music-theoretical pursuits—the analysis of equal-tempered systems. In two earlier articles I discussed certain of their structural aspects[1]; then, in preparing a series of lectures on this subject given at Princeton University in the spring of 1974, I discovered some further resources of such systems that prior to then had not been subject to theoretical investigation. This chapter is based on the Princeton lectures.

The literature on equal-tempered systems is a large and continually expanding subcategory of the literature on microtonal, or xenharmonic, systems in general. To survey it would take me beyond the limits of this study.[2] Much of the literature is concerned with tuning and temperament, and particularly with the relationship of the frequency ratios of various equal-tempered systems to the ratios of just intonation. This is a problem of great importance, to which I shall return later. First of all, however, I

1. Carlton Gamer, "Some Combinational Resources of Equal-Tempered Systems," *Journal of Music Theory* 11, no. 1 (1967): 32–59; idem, "Deep Scales and Difference Sets in Equal-Tempered Systems," *Proceedings of the American Society of University Composers* 2 (1967): 113–122.

2. For useful surveys of the field, see J. Murray Barbour, *Tuning and Temperament: A Historical Survey* (East Lansing: Michigan State College Press, 1953) and Joel Mandelbaum, "Multiple Division of the Octave and the Tonal Resources of 19-Tone Temperament" (Ph.D. dissertation, Indiana University, 1961). An essential recent work is Eric Regener, *Pitch Notation and Equal Temperament: A Formal Study* (Berkeley: University of California Press, 1973).

MUSIC THEORY: SPECIAL TOPICS

should like to consider some rather different aspects of the subject and, in so doing, explore some systems not usually dealt with in the existing sources.

To begin with a definition: An *equal-tempered system,* or *ETS,* means a set of n tones filling the span of an octave, arranged scalewise in the order of their increasing fundamental frequencies so that the common ratio of the fundamental frequency of any tone in the system to that of the next is $1: \sqrt[n]{2}$. The pitch of each tone in an ETS is to be regarded as representative of a pitch class. Pitch-class membership is defined by octave equivalence, whereby a member of a given pitch class differs from each other member of that class by an integral number of octaves. The successive pitch classes of an ETS of n tones are denoted by the integer notation 0, 1, 2, . . ., $n - 1$. An ETS of n tones will be abbreviated "ETS n."

The aspects of ETSs I have found most intriguing, and with which I shall be dealing primarily in this chapter, are those most directly related to my interests as a composer of music in ETS 12. In recent years these interests have centered more and more upon the attainment in the pitch domain of a sense of "less-than-twelveness" embedded in "twelveness." I have become increasingly preoccupied with the properties of certain subcollections of pitches or pitch classes chosen from the universe of pitches within our system and the relationships of such subcollections to that system.

Subcollections of ETS 12

Two types of subcollection of ETS 12 have seemed to me to be of particular compositional significance. The first of these types is that termed by Babbitt a *maximal subcollection*[3] or by Winograd and me a *deep scale.*[4]

The Deep Scale

The *deep scale* is a pitch-class set characterized by an interval vector showing each interval class in the system represented with unique multiplicity, as a consequence of which the set of transpositions of the subcol-

3. In Milton Babbitt, "Twelve-Tone Rhythmic Structure and the Electronic Medium," *Perspectives of New Music* 1, no. 1 (1962): 49–79, pp. 76–77. See also Babbitt, "The Structure and Function of Music Theory: I," *College Music Symposium* 5 (1965): 49–60, p. 54.

4. See Gamer, "Combinational Resources," pp. 39–46, and "Deep Scales," pp. 119–120; and for detailed analysis and proofs of theorems relating to such scales, see Terry Winograd, "An Analysis of the Properties of Deep Scales in a T-Tone System" (unpublished ms.).

lection can be hierarchically ordered in terms of the common tone relationship of its various members to any one referential member.

Four such deep scales exist within ETS 12: [0, 1, 2, 3, 4, 5] (Forte 6–1), [0, 1, 2, 3, 4, 5, 6] (Forte 7–1), [0, 2, 4, 5, 7, 9] (Forte 6–32), and [0, 1, 3, 5, 6, 8, 10] (Forte 7–35),[5] with respective interval vectors [5 4 3 2 1 0], [6 5 4 3 2 1], [1 4 3 2 5 0], and [2 5 4 3 6 1].

This type of subcollection and its properties are by now well known both to students of twelve-tone theory and of the theory of tonal music.

The Difference Set

Of related interest is that type of subcollection that might be termed a *difference set;* that is, a pitch-class set characterized by an interval vector showing all interval classes in the system represented with equal multiplicity. In ETS 12, the set of transpositions of such a subcollection cannot, of course, be hierarchically ordered in terms of common tone relationships; rather, its most significant property is that each pair of pitch classes in the system (with the exception of those pairs whose members lie a tritone apart) is defined by membership in one and only one transposition.

Two such difference sets exist in ETS 12, namely the so-called "all-interval tetrads" [0, 1, 4, 6] (Forte 4–Z15) and [0, 1, 3, 7] (Forte 4–Z29), each with interval vector [1 1 1 1 1 1].

Consider the following array of transpositions generated by the difference set [0, 1, 4, 6] (Figure 3.1):[6]

(0, 1, 4, 6)	(6, 7, 10, 0)
(1, 2, 5, 7)	(7, 8, 11, 1)
(2, 3, 6, 8)	(8, 9, 0, 2)
(3, 4, 7, 9)	(9, 10, 1, 3)
(4, 5, 8, 10)	(10, 11, 2, 4)
(5, 6, 9, 11)	(11, 0, 3, 5)

FIGURE 3.1

5. The citation following each collection refers to the set name assigned to it by Forte. See Allen Forte, *The Structure of Atonal Music* (New Haven: Yale University Press, 1973), Appendix 1, pp. 179–181.

6. Unless otherwise indicated, brackets [ ] will be used to enclose the prime form of a *pitch-structure class* (a concept to be introduced on page 66) or to enclose the interval vector of such a form. Parentheses ( ) will be used to enclose pitch-class sets that are transpositionally or inversionally equivalent to a given prime form. Regarding prime form, interval vector, and transpositional and inversional equivalence, see Forte, *Structure of Atonal Music*, Glossary of Technical Terms, pp. 209–211

It can be seen that of the 66 pairs of pitch classes in ETS 12, 60 pairs appear once each; that is, in one and only one transposition. The remaining 6 pairs, whose pitch-class numbers yield a difference of 6 (mod 12)—the pairs (0, 6), (1, 7), (2, 8), (3, 9), (4, 10), (5, 11)—appear twice each, in two transpositions a tritone apart.

The same distribution of pairs of pitch classes is found in the transpositions of the other difference set, [0, 1, 3, 7], 60 pairs appearing in one and only one transposition, the remaining 6 pairs, as enumerated above, appearing in two.

Thus it can be seen that no set of transpositions can be generated by either of the difference sets in ETS 12 such that each pair of pitch classes appears once and only once in the set. In other words, no *cyclic block design* exists in ETS 12. This concept will be explained presently.

Subcollections of Other ETSs

My initial exploration of ETSs other than ETS 12 was prompted by my observation that in certain other systems both deep scales and difference sets were to be found not only in greater variety and profusion than in our own, but, especially in the case of difference sets, possessing more significant properties as well.

The Deep Scale

Deep scales, of course, are to be found in every ETS, as a pair of such subcollections can be generated by any interval the size of which is relatively prime to the number of tones in the ETS. Therefore, in ETSs containing, for example, a prime number of tones, a pair of deep scales can be generated by every interval in the system.

The Difference Set

As for difference sets, these are not to be found in every ETS. However, in certain ETSs in which one or more such sets are to be found they can be seen to possess a property not characteristic of the difference sets in ETS 12, namely that they can each generate a *cyclic block design*. Moreover, in certain ETSs there exist extensions or refinements of the concept of the difference set. For example, an extension of the concept is the idea of a *difference set complex;* and a refinement of the concept is the idea of a difference set in which are represented with equal multiplicity not merely each of the interval classes of the system—that is, *pitch-struc-*

ture classes of cardinality 2—but at the same time each of the triad classes or other *pitch-structure classes* of cardinality greater than 2.

BLOCK DESIGNS

By a *block design* is meant a system of n tones and b transpositions, or *blocks,* such that each transposition contains the same number, k, of tones, each tone is in the same number, r, of transpositions, and each pair of pitch classes appears in the same number, λ, of transpositions.

By a *cyclic block design* is meant a block design with parameters such that $n = b$, $k = r$, and "given any block B_i, each of the other blocks can be obtained by adding one of the residues (mod n) 1,2, . . ., $n - 1$ to each member of B_i."[7]

Rahn[8] has shown that the relationship among parameters in any cyclic block design is as follows:

$$b \cdot \binom{k}{2} = \lambda \cdot \binom{n}{2} \qquad \text{where } \binom{n}{m} \text{ denotes } \frac{n!}{m!(n-m)!} \qquad (3.1)$$

Of particular musical interest is the cyclic block design with parameters $n = b$, $k = r$, and $\lambda = 1$. This design can be generated only by a difference set containing a single representative of each of the interval classes in the ETS.

The conditions on the existence of such a design within an ETS are these: First, that the number of tones in the system be an odd number; second, that the number of interval classes in the system be a triangular number—that is, one of the series 1, 3, 6, 10, 15, 21, . . .; and third, that a difference set of the type just specified exist within the system to function as the block design generator. It can be seen, then, that no cyclic block design with parameters $n = b$, $k = r$, and $\lambda = 1$ exists in ETS 12— as was demonstrated above—because although the second and third conditions are met, the first is not. Nor does this cyclic block design exist, for example, in ETS 43, for whereas the first two conditions are met, the third is not; here, no difference set exists that contains a representative of each of the 21 interval classes in the system.[9] But in a number of ETSs cyclic block designs of this kind are to be found, as well as other kinds of block design (to be introduced presently) the parameters of which will vary in accordance with the properties of the generator.

7. Winograd, "Properties of Deep Scales," p. 5.

8. John Rahn of the University of Washington School of Music, in private communication.

9. For an explanation of this see page 69.

TABLE 3.1
ETS 11

PITCH CLASSES: 0, 1, 2, 3, 4, 5, 6, 7, 8, 9, 10
NUMBER OF INTERVAL CLASSES: 5, the prime forms of which are as follows: [0, 1]   [0, 2]
[0, 3]   [0, 4]   [0, 5]
CARDINALITY OF DEEP SCALES: 5 or 6

DEEP SCALES OF CARDINALITY 5:

Generator	Deep scale	Interval vector
1	[0, 1, 2, 3, 4]	[4 3 2 1 0]
2	[0, 2, 4, 6, 8]	[0 4 1 3 2]
3	[0, 2, 3, 5, 8]	[1 2 4 0 3]
4	[0, 1, 4, 5, 8]	[2 0 3 4 1]
5	[0, 1, 2, 6, 7]	[3 1 0 2 4]

DEEP SCALES OF CARDINALITY 6:

Generator	Deep scale	Interval vector
1	[0, 1, 2, 3, 4, 5]	[5 4 3 2 1]
2	[0, 1, 3, 5, 7, 9]	[1 5 2 4 3]
3	[0, 2, 3, 5, 6, 8]	[2 3 5 1 4]
4	[0, 1, 3, 4, 7, 8]	[3 1 4 5 2]
5	[0, 1, 2, 5, 6, 7]	[4 2 1 3 5]

DIFFERENCE SET CONTAINING A SINGLE REPRESENTATIVE OF EACH INTERVAL CLASS:
none
NUMBER OF TRIAD CLASSES: 10, the prime forms of which are as follows: [0, 1, 2]   [0, 1, 3]
[0, 1, 4]   [0, 1, 5]   [0, 1, 6]   [0, 2, 4]   [0, 2, 5]   [0, 2, 6]   [0, 3, 6]   [0, 3, 7]
DIFFERENCE SET CONTAINING A SINGLE REPRESENTATIVE OF EACH TRIAD CLASS:

Difference set	Interval vector
[0, 1, 2, 4, 7]	[2 2 2 2 2]

CYCLIC BLOCK DESIGN WITH PARAMETERS $n = b = 11$, $k = r = 5$, $\lambda = 2$, GENERATED
BY THE DIFFERENCE SET [0, 1, 2, 4, 7]:

(0, 1, 2, 4, 7)	(6, 7, 8, 10, 2)
(1, 2, 3, 5, 8)	(7, 8, 9, 0, 3)
(2, 3, 4, 6, 9)	(8, 9, 10, 1, 4)
(3, 4, 5, 7, 10)	(9, 10, 0, 2, 5)
(4, 5, 6, 8, 0)	(10, 0, 1, 3, 6)
(5, 6, 7, 9, 1)	

NUMBER OF TETRAD CLASSES: 20
DIFFERENCE SET CONTAINING A SINGLE REPRESENTATIVE OF EACH TETRAD CLASS:
none
PERIOD OF EACH NONZERO INTERVAL UNDER ADDITION (mod 11):   11
PERIOD OF EACH NONZERO INTERVAL UNDER MULTIPLICATION (mod 11):

Interval	Period	Interval	Period
1	1	6	10
2	10	7	10
3	5	8	10
4	5	9	5
5	5	10	2

TABLE 3.2
ETS 13

PITCH CLASSES: 0, 1, 2, 3, 4, 5, 6, 7, 8, 9, 10, 11, 12

NUMBER OF INTERVAL CLASSES: 6, the prime forms of which are as follows: [0, 1]
[0, 2] [0, 3] [0, 4] [0, 5] [0, 6]

CARDINALITY OF DEEP SCALES: 6 or 7

DEEP SCALES OF CARDINALITY 6:

Generator	Deep scale	Interval vector
1	[0, 1, 2, 3, 4, 5]	[5 4 3 2 1 0]
2	[0, 2, 4, 6, 8, 10]	[0 5 1 4 2 3]
3	[0, 1, 3, 4, 7, 10]	[2 1 5 3 0 4]
4	[0, 1, 4, 5, 8, 9]	[3 0 2 5 4 1]
5	[0, 2, 3, 5, 8, 10]	[1 3 4 0 5 2]
6	[0, 1, 2, 6, 7, 8]	[4 2 0 1 3 5]

DEEP SCALES OF CARDINALITY 7:

Generator	Deep scale	Interval vector
1	[0, 1, 2, 3, 4, 5, 6]	[6 5 4 3 2 1]
2	[0, 1, 3, 5, 7, 9, 11]	[1 6 2 5 3 4]
3	[0, 1, 3, 4, 7, 10, 11]	[3 2 6 4 1 5]
4	[0, 1, 2, 5, 6, 9, 10]	[4 1 3 6 5 2]
5	[0, 1, 3, 6, 8, 9, 11]	[2 4 5 1 6 3]
6	[0, 1, 2, 3, 7, 8, 9]	[5 3 1 2 4 6]

DIFFERENCE SETS CONTAINING A SINGLE REPRESENTATIVE OF EACH INTERVAL CLASS: 2, as follows:

Difference set	Interval vector
[0, 1, 4, 6]	[1 1 1 1 1 1]
[0, 2, 3, 7]	[1 1 1 1 1 1]

CYCLIC BLOCK DESIGN WITH PARAMETERS $n = b = 13$, $k = r = 4$, $\lambda = 1$, GENERATED BY THE DIFFERENCE SET [0, 1, 4, 6]:

(0, 1, 4, 6)	(7, 8, 11, 0)
(1, 2, 5, 7)	(8, 9, 12, 1)
(2, 3, 6, 8)	(9, 10, 0, 2)
(3, 4, 7, 9)	(10, 11, 1, 3)
(4, 5, 8, 10)	(11, 12, 2, 4)
(5, 6, 9, 11)	(12, 0, 3, 5)
(6, 7, 10, 12)	

DIFFERENCE SET COMPLEX: [[0, 1, 4][0, 2, 7]]

BLOCK DESIGN WITH PARAMETERS $n = 13$, $b = 26$, $k = 3$, $r = 6$, $\lambda = 1$, GENERATED BY THE DIFFERENCE SET COMPLEX [[0, 1, 4][0, 2, 7]]:

(0, 1, 4)(0, 2, 7)	(7, 8, 11)(7, 9, 1)
(1, 2, 5)(1, 3, 8)	(8, 9, 12)(8, 10, 2)
(2, 3, 6)(2, 4, 9)	(9, 10, 0)(9, 11, 3)
(3, 4, 7)(3, 5, 10)	(10, 11, 1)(10, 12, 4)
(4, 5, 8)(4, 6, 11)	(11, 12, 2)(11, 0, 5)
(5, 6, 9)(5, 7, 12)	(12, 0, 3)(12, 1, 6)
(6, 7, 10)(6, 8, 0)	

TABLE 3.2 (*continued*)

NUMBER OF TRIAD CLASSES: 14
DIFFERENCE SET CONTAINING A SINGLE REPRESENTATIVE OF EACH TRIAD CLASS:
    none
NUMBER OF TETRAD CLASSES: 35
DIFFERENCE SET CONTAINING A SINGLE REPRESENTATIVE OF EACH TETRAD CLASS:
    none
PERIOD OF EACH NONZERO INTERVAL UNDER ADDITION (mod 13): 13
PERIOD OF EACH NONZERO INTERVAL UNDER MULTIPLICATION (mod 13):

Interval	Period	Interval	Period
1	1	7	12
2	12	8	4
3	3	9	3
4	6	10	6
5	4	11	12
6	12	12	2

THE DIFFERENCE SET COMPLEX

By a *difference set complex* is meant a set of pitch-class sets in an ETS such that the entire complex has the property, previously mentioned in regard to the difference set, of containing all interval classes in the system with equal multiplicity.

PITCH-STRUCTURE CLASSES

By a *pitch-structure class* (or *"PS" class*) of cardinality j is meant the set of all pitch-class sets transpositionally or inversionally equivalent to a given pitch-class set of cardinality j. Such a PS class can always be represented by one of its members, traditionally that normally ordered member that might be termed the *prime form*, or *prototype*, of the pitch-class set. Thus in ETS 12 there are six PS classes of cardinality 2—that is, the six interval classes; 12 PS classes of cardinality 3—the 12 triad classes; 29 of cardinality 4—the 29 tetrad classes; and so on.[10]

The concepts I have just introduced—the deep scale, the difference set, the block design, the difference set complex, and the difference set containing representatives of PS classes of cardinality greater than 2—can each be illustrated by reference to ETS 11 or ETS 13. The salient features of these systems are shown in Tables 3.1 and 3.2.

10. In Forte, *Structure of Atonal Music,* Appendix 1, pp. 179–181, are listed the prime forms and interval vectors of every PS class of cardinality 3–9 in ETS 12.

ETS 11 and ETS 13

Deep Scales in ETS 11 and ETS 13

To begin with deep scales, it can be seen in the tables that the cardinality of each of these is a function of the number of interval classes in the ETS. For a given ETS n in which n is even, the number of interval classes is equal to $n/2$; where n is odd, $(n - 1)/2$. For ETSs of any size, this formula can be abbreviated to $[n/2]$, the bracket here denoting the largest integer not greater than $n/2$. The cardinality of each of the deep scales in an ETS, then, is equal either to $[n/2]$ or $[n/2] + 1$.

As mentioned above, in ETSs where the number of tones in the system is a prime number, each interval in the system can function as the generator of two deep scales. The normally ordered forms of such subcollections in ETS 11 and ETS 13 are shown in the tables, together with the generator and interval vector of each. (For the sake of brevity, not all intervals in each system are shown as generators. The generators listed are only those intervals which are interval *classes* in the system.) Note that the interval vector of each subcollection of cardinality $[n/2] + 1$ can be obtained by adding 1 to the value of each term in the interval vector of the corresponding subcollection of cardinality $[n/2]$.

Difference Sets in ETS 11 and ETS 13

With regard to difference sets containing a representative of each interval class, it can be seen that ETS 11 contains no such set, whereas ETS 13 contains two. ETS 11 contains five interval classes; ETS 13 contains six. These six interval classes, like the six interval classes in ETS 12, can be contained in either of two difference sets of cardinality 4. And like the difference sets of cardinality 4 in ETS 12, which are equivalent under the multiplicative operations M5 or M7 (mod 12), the difference sets in ETS 13 are also equivalent under certain multiplicative operations, these being M2, M5, or M6 (mod 13).

BLOCK DESIGNS

Note that each of the difference sets in ETS 13, unlike those in ETS 12, can generate a cyclic block design. One of these designs, that generated by the difference set [0, 1, 4, 6], is shown in Table 3.2. Compare this with the array of transpositions generated by the same difference set in ETS 12, as shown in Figure 3.1. It can be seen that in ETS 13 each of the 78 pairs of pitch classes in the system appears once and only once in the cyclic block design.

THE DIFFERENCE SET COMPLEX

ETS 13 also serves to illustrate the concept of the difference set complex, a compositional resource not found in ETS 12. Within the two triads of the complex are contained a single representative of each of the six interval classes of the system. From this difference set complex can be generated a block design differing somewhat from the cyclic block design introduced earlier, wherein $n = b$ and $k = r$. Here the block is to be regarded as a triad. The block design, then, consists of 13 triad pairs. Thus the relationship among parameters is such that $n \neq b$ and $k \neq r$. Note, however, that once again $\lambda = 1$; that is, each of the 78 pairs of pitch classes in the system appears in one and only one block.

PITCH–STRUCTURE CLASSES

We come now to a consideration of PS classes of cardinality greater than 2. Referring to Table 3.1, we see that ETS 11 contains exactly 10 triad classes. A representative of each of these 10 triad classes can be contained in one "all-triad pentad" analogous to the "all-interval tetrads" of ETS 12 or ETS 13. This all-triad pentad is also a difference set, but of a different order than that of the all-interval tetrads. (Note that in the interval vector of this pentad—as in that of the tetrads—each interval class of the system occurs with equal multiplicity; here, however, the multiplicity of occurrence of each is two rather than one.) From the fact that it contains a representative of each of the 10 triad classes in ETS 11, it follows that this pentad can generate a block design, also shown in Table 3.1, in which each of the 11 transpositions of each of these class representatives will appear in one and only one block.

In any ETS, a necessary condition on the existence of a difference set of cardinality i containing a representative of each PS class of cardinality j is this: that the number of PS classes of cardinality j be a binomial coefficient of order i. For convenient reference, the table of binomial coefficients through order 7 is given in Figure 3.2.

As we have already seen, a representative of each of the six interval classes of ETS 12 or ETS 13 can be contained in a difference set of cardinality 4, 6 being a binomial coefficient of order 4. Likewise, a representative of each of the 15 interval classes of ETS 31—a very important system to which I shall return in the last section—can be contained in any of a number of difference sets of cardinality 6.

And, as we have just observed in Table 3.1, the 10 triad classes of ETS 11 can each be represented in a difference set of cardinality 5. However, as noted in Tables 3.1 and 3.2, neither the five interval classes of ETS 11 nor the 14 triad classes of ETS 13 can be represented in a difference set of

i	$j = 0$	1 (pitch classes)	2 (interval classes)	3 (triad classes)	4 (tetrad classes)	5 (pentad classes)	6 (hexad classes)	7 (heptad classes)
0	1							
1	1	1						
2	1	2	1					
3	1	3	3	1				
4	1	4	6	4	1			
5	1	5	10	10	5	1		
6	1	6	15	20	15	6	1	
7	1	7	21	35	35	21	7	1

FIGURE 3.2. Binomial coefficients.

any size; 5 does not appear in the interval class column and 14 does not appear in the triad class column of Figure 3.2.

The condition just mentioned on the existence of a difference set within an ETS is a necessary but not a sufficient one. Later on in Table 3.2 it is noted that the 35 tetrad classes of ETS 13 can *not* each be represented in a difference set. Despite the fact that 35 appears in the tetrad column of Figure 3.2, no difference set of cardinality 7 exists. Neither is there a difference set of cardinality 7, as observed earlier, containing a representative of each of the 21 interval classes of ETS 43.[11] A condition on the existence of a difference set of cardinality i containing a representative of each of the interval classes in an ETS is that i be of the form $i = p^t + 1$, where p is prime and t is an integer. Thus 7 is excluded as a value of i.

Because in dealing with difference sets containing representatives of PS classes of cardinality greater than 2 it is essential to know how many such classes exist in a given ETS, it is helpful to have a formula, or formulas, for determining this. Of particular value are the formulas for determining the number of triad and tetrad classes in an ETS. Janke[12] has shown that the formula for the number of triad classes (C_3) in an ETS of n tones is as follows (brackets once again denoting the greatest integer):

$$C_3 = \frac{1}{2}\left(\left[\frac{\{(n^2 - 3n + 2)/2\} + 2}{3}\right] + \left[\frac{n-1}{2}\right]\right) \qquad (3.2)$$

11. Regarding the problem of the cyclic block design with parameters $n = b = 43$, $k = r = 7$, and $\lambda = 1$, see the discussion of the Bruck–Ryser–Chowla Theorem in Marshall Hall, Jr., *Combinatorial Theory* (Waltham, Massachusetts: Blaisdell Publishing Co., 1967), chap. 10, sect. 10.3, pp. 107–109.

12. Steven Janke of The Colorado College Department of Mathematics, in private communication.

The formulas for the number of tetrad classes (C_4) are as follows:

Let

$$T = \frac{(n - 1)(n - 2)(n - 3)}{6}$$

$$D = \left[\frac{n}{4}\right]$$

$$S = \frac{1}{2}\left[\frac{n - 2}{2}\right]\left(\left[\frac{n - 2}{2}\right] + 1\right)$$

Then if n is odd,

$$C_4 = \frac{1}{2}\left(\frac{T}{4} + S\right) \tag{3.3}$$

If n is even but not divisible by 4,

$$C_4 = \frac{1}{2}\left(\frac{T - 2D}{4} + D + S\right) \tag{3.4}$$

If n is even and divisible by 4,

$$C_4 = \frac{1}{2}\left(\frac{T - 2D + 1}{4} + D + S\right) \tag{3.5}$$

One further aspect of the subject of PS classes should be considered at this point, namely that definitions of such classes other than the definition I have given on page 66 are possible. Among several alternatives, two immediately suggest themselves: first, that membership in a PS class be limited to transpositionally equivalent pitch-class sets only, excluding inversional equivalence as a criterion; or second—in contrast to the first alternative—that membership be expanded to include not only all pitch-class sets that are the transpositional or inversional equivalents of a given pitch-class set, but also all pitch-class sets that are the transpositional or inversional equivalents of the *product* of some multiplicative operation Mp upon this given set, where p is any number which is relatively prime to the number of tones in the ETS. (Here the significant values of p, in an ETS of n tones, are those values other than 1 or $n - 1$. Of course, $M1$ is the identity operation upon a set, and $M(n - 1)$ yields its inversion.)

The first of these alternatives agrees with Howe's definition of what he terms *pitch structure*.[13] While limiting the number of members in each PS class, this definition increases the total number of PS classes in a given ETS. The second of these alternatives agrees with Starr and Morris's definition of what they term *set class*[14]; it has the opposite effect: While increasing the number of members in each PS class, the definition limits the total number of PS classes in a given ETS.

As an example of each of these effects, consider the triad classes in ETS 12. In accordance with my initial definition of PS class, 12 such triad classes exist in ETS 12. In accordance with the first alternative, this number increases to 19. In accordance with the second, where in addition to transpositional or inversional equivalence—that is, equivalence under M1 or M11 (mod 12)—equivalence under M5 or M7 (mod 12) becomes a criterion for class membership, this number decreases to 9.

From the standpoint of the theory under discussion, certain positive or negative consequences might result from the adoption of either of the alternative definitions of PS class just mentioned. On the one hand, the number of PS classes of cardinality j within a given ETS might prove to be a binomial coefficient of order i. On the other hand, if there exists therefore a set of cardinality i containing a representative of each of these PS classes, this set might prove not to be a difference set.

Consider, for example, ETS 8 and the question of the number of triad classes it contains. In accordance with my initial definition of PS class, there are five triad classes in ETS 8, the prime forms of which are as follows: [0, 1, 2], [0, 1, 3], [0, 1, 4], [0, 2, 4], and [0, 2, 5]. Now consider the normally ordered products of the multiplicative operations $M3$ or $M5$ (mod 8) upon each of these forms, as follows (Figure 3.3). Note that [0, 1, 2] and [0, 2, 5] are equivalent under M5.

If we now adopt the second alternative definition of PS class, whereby in addition to equivalence under M1 or M7 (mod 8) equivalence under $M3$ or $M5$ (mod 8) becomes a criterion for class membership, there are only

M5: [0, 1, 2] → [0, 2, 5]
M3: [0, 1, 3] → [0, 1, 3]
M5: [0, 1, 4] → [0, 1, 4]
M3: [0, 2, 4] → [0, 2, 4]
M5: [0, 2, 5] → [0, 1, 2]

FIGURE 3.3.

13. See Hubert Howe, "Some Combinational Properties of Pitch Structures," *Perspectives of New Music* 4, no. 1 (1965): 45–61, p. 49.

14. See Daniel Starr and Robert Morris, "A General Theory of Combinatoriality and the Aggregate (Part I)," *Perspectives of New Music* 16, no. 1 (1977): 3–35, p. 11.

four triad classes, the prime forms of which are as follows: [0, 1, 2], [0, 1, 3], [0, 1, 4], and [0, 2, 4].

Since 4 is a binomial coefficient of order 4, we can therefore test for the existence in ETS 8 of a set of cardinality 4 containing a representative of each of these triad classes. The set proves to be [0, 1, 2, 4]. This set, however, is of course not a difference set, as its interval vector, [2 2 1 1], does not show each interval class in ETS 8 represented with equal multiplicity.

(It is of interest that this same set, [0, 1, 2, 4], *does* function as a difference set in ETS 7. Since in ETS 7 there exist only three interval classes rather than four, the interval vector of this set in that system is [2 2 2], as shown in Table 3.3.)

Because of certain problematic consequences of the adoption of either of the two alternative definitions I have just discussed—or of other alternative definitions not mentioned—I have decided to adhere in this article to the initial definition of PS class given on page 66.

Periods of Intervals

In gauging the compositional potential of a given ETS it is necessary to determine the *period* of each of the various intervals in the system. In this regard, ETS 11 and ETS 13 serve as an instructive contrast to ETS 12.

The Period of an Interval Under Addition

By an interval is meant the absolute value of the difference between the integers denoting any two pitch classes in an ETS of n tones. The n intervals in an n-tone ETS constitute a finite group under the binary operation of addition, with the interval 0 as the group identity element.[15] Let a be an element of this group, and let the powers of a under addition be defined as follows: $a^0 = 0$ (identity); $a^1 = a$; $a^2 = a + a$; $a^3 = a + a + a$; . . . $a^n = 0 \pmod{n}$. Then the least positive integer t for which $a^t = 0 \pmod{n}$ is the *period* of a under addition. Thus in ETS 12 the period of the intervals 1, 5, 7, and 11 is 12; of 2 and 10, 6; of 3 and 9, 4; of 4 and 8, 3; and of 6, 2.

The variety of periodicities of its intervals under addition is one of the attractive features of ETS 12. By contrast, any ETS of n tones where n is a prime number, as in ETS 11 or ETS 13, is relatively impoverished in

---

15. For a discussion of the group postulates as these apply to the intervals in an ETS, see Gamer, "Combinational Resources," pp. 36–39.

terms of the variety of periodicities of its intervals under addition; here, the periods of all intervals in the system are the same, each being equal to n.

The Period of an Interval Under Multiplication

The situation is quite different, however, if a is regarded as an element of a finite group under the binary operation of multiplication, with the interval 1 as the group identity element. Now let the powers of a under multiplication be defined as follows: $a^0 = 1$ (identity); $a^1 = a$; $a^2 = a \times a$; $a^3 = a \times a \times a$; . . . $a^n = 1$ (mod n), and let the *period* of a be defined as the least positive integer t for which $a^t = 1$ (mod n).

The intervals in ETS 12 that constitute a finite group under multiplication are only four in number, not 12 in number as is the case under addition. These four are the *totitives* of 12—i.e., the nonzero intervals relatively prime to 12—1, 5, 7, and 11. Under multiplication the period of 1 is 1; and of 5, 7, and 11, 2. [The eight remaining nontotitive intervals do not belong to or constitute a group under multiplication because, being by definition factors of 12, none has an integral inverse i such that $a \times i = 1$ (identity); as a corollary of this, for none of these intervals does there exist a positive integer t for which $a^t = 1$ (mod 12).] Thus, under multiplication no interval in ETS 12 has a period greater than 2.

In an ETS of n tones where n is a prime number, however, every nonzero interval is a totitive of n, and therefore all such intervals in the ETS constitute a finite group. Furthermore, we find in ETSs where n is prime a variety of periodicities of intervals under multiplication which is analogous to the variety found in ETS 12 under addition. As an illustration of this, the period of each of the intervals in ETS 11 and ETS 13 under multiplication is shown in Tables 3.1 and 3.2.

Multiplicative Operations

In an ETS of n tones, any interval which is a totitive of n can function as a *multiplicative operator* M_p on any pitch-class set in the system. The period of the operator is a determining factor in the number of successive mappings whereby the operand will yield itself under the operation. In ETS 12, as we have seen, this number can never be greater than 2; for example, the two successive mappings whereby the pitch-class set [0, 1, 3] will yield itself under $M5$ (mod 12) are these (transposed to 0): $(0, 1, 3) \rightarrow (0, 3, 5) \rightarrow (0, 1, 3)$. Now consider the successive mappings of the same pitch-class set, [0, 1, 3] under the operator $M5$ (mod 11) in ETS 11. Here the interval 5 has a period of 5 under multiplication, as shown in

Table 3.1, and the mappings whereby this set will yield itself in ETS 11 are also 5 in number, as follows (transposed to 0): $(0, 1, 3) \rightarrow (0, 4, 5) \rightarrow$ $(0, 2, 5) \rightarrow (0, 1, 4) \rightarrow (0, 4, 6) \rightarrow (0, 1, 3)$.

(Another determining factor in the number of mappings is the interval vector of the operand itself. A difference set, for example, with interval vector $[1 \ 1 \ . \ . \ . \ 1]$, might under certain conditions map directly into itself, as is the case with the difference set $[0, 1, 4, 6]$ under $M3$ (mod 13) in ETS 13. Despite the fact that here the period of the interval 3 is 3, as shown in Table 3.2, the mapping is $(0, 1, 4, 6) \rightarrow (0, 1, 4, 6)$.)

It should be noted that the periods of the intervals 10 in ETS 11, 11 in ETS 12, and 12 in ETS 13 are all 2. In general, for any value of n greater than 1, $(n - 1)^2 = 1 \pmod{n}$. Since $M(n - 1)$ is the inversion operation in an ETS of n tones, it follows that in any ETS the number of successive mappings whereby a given pitch-class set will yield itself under inversion will always be 2.

I shall now turn from a theoretical consideration of multiplicative operations to a compositional application.

A Composition in ETS 7

ETS 7 will serve not only to illustrate some aspects of multiplicative operations but also to exemplify virtually every other concept that has been discussed so far. The relevant properties of this system are summarized in Table 3.3.

While many of the combinational resources of ETS 7 are of compositional interest, I have availed myself of one in particular as the basis for a short piece of music. This resource is the maximally large period (6) of the intervals 3 or 5 under multiplication, which determines the maximally large number of mappings (6) whereby each interval class will yield itself under M3 or M5 (mod 7). In this piece, M3 is the operator.

The syntactic model of which the piece is an interpretation consists of a series of six mappings of a triad, $[0, 1, 4]$, rather than of an interval class. This model, which was proposed by J.K. Randall of Princeton University, is shown in Figure 3.4.

If the triad $[0, 1, 4]$ is regarded as a sonority, it can be heard as consisting of the foundation interval 1, denoted by the integer notation 0 1, upon which is superimposed an interval three times its size, namely the interval 3, denoted by the integer notation 1..4. (The two dots here denote the implied pitch classes defining the unit intervals that comprise the upper interval.) The pitch classes defining the upper interval are then taken to

TABLE 3.3
ETS 7

PITCH CLASSES: 0, 1, 2, 3, 4, 5, 6
NUMBER OF INTERVAL CLASSES: 3, the prime forms of which are as follows: [0, 1] [0, 2]
  [0, 3]
CARDINALITY OF DEEP SCALES: 3 or 4
DEEP SCALES OF CARDINALITY 3:

Generator	Deep scale	Interval vector
1	[0, 1, 2]	[2 1 0]
2	[0, 2, 4]	[0 2 1]
3	[0, 1, 4]	[1 0 2]

DEEP SCALES OF CARDINALITY 4:

Generator	Deep scale	Interval vector
1	[0, 1, 2, 3]	[3 2 1]
2	[0, 1, 3, 5]	[1 3 2]
3	[0, 1, 3, 4]	[2 1 3]

DIFFERENCE SET CONTAINING A SINGLE REPRESENTATIVE OF EACH INTERVAL CLASS:

Difference set	Interval vector
[0, 1, 3]	[1 1 1]

CYCLIC BLOCK DESIGN WITH PARAMETERS $n = b = 7$, $k = r = 3$, $\lambda = 1$, GENERATED BY
THE DIFFERENCE SET [0, 1, 3]:

(0, 1, 3)	(4, 5, 0)
(1, 2, 4)	(5, 6, 1)
(2, 3, 5)	(6, 0, 2)
(3, 4, 6)	

NUMBER OF TRIAD CLASSES: 4, the prime forms of which are as follows: [0, 1, 2]
  [0, 1, 3] [0, 1, 4] [0, 2, 4]
DIFFERENCE SET CONTAINING A SINGLE REPRESENTATIVE OF EACH TRIAD CLASS:

Difference set	Interval vector
[0, 1, 2, 4]	[2 2 2]

CYCLIC BLOCK DESIGN WITH PARAMETERS $n = b = 7$, $k = r = 4$, $\lambda = 2$, GENERATED BY
THE DIFFERENCE SET [0, 1, 2, 4]:

(0, 1, 2, 4)	(4, 5, 6, 1)
(1, 2, 3, 5)	(5, 6, 0, 2)
(2, 3, 4, 6)	(6, 0, 1, 3)
(3, 4, 5, 0)	

PERIOD OF EACH NONZERO INTERVAL UNDER ADDITION (mod 7): 7

PERIOD OF EACH NONZERO INTERVAL UNDER MULTIPLICATION (mod 7):

Interval	Period	Interval	Period
1	1	4	3
2	3	5	6
3	6	6	2

TABLE 3.3 *(continued)*

M-OPERATIONS ON INTERVAL CLASSES:

Operator	Operand	Mappings
*M*2:	[0, 1]	(0, 1) → (0, 2) → (0, 4) → (0, 1)
	[0, 2]	(0, 2) → (0, 4) → (0, 1) → (0, 2)
	[0, 3]	(0, 3) → (0, 6) → (0, 5) → (0, 3)
*M*3:	[0, 1]	(0, 1) → (0, 3) → (0, 2) → (0, 6) → (0, 4) → (0, 5) → (0, 1)
	[0, 2]	(0, 2) → (0, 6) → (0, 4) → (0, 5) → (0, 1) → (0, 3) → (0, 2)
	[0, 3]	(0, 3) → (0, 2) → (0, 6) → (0, 4) → (0, 5) → (0, 1) → (0, 3)
*M*4:	[0, 1]	(0, 1) → (0, 4) → (0, 2) → (0, 1)
	[0, 2]	(0, 2) → (0, 1) → (0, 4) → (0, 2)
	[0, 3]	(0, 3) → (0, 5) → (0, 6) → (0, 3)
*M*5:	[0, 1]	(0, 1) → (0, 5) → (0, 4) → (0, 6) → (0, 2) → (0, 3) → (0, 1)
	[0, 2]	(0, 2) → (0, 3) → (0, 1) → (0, 5) → (0, 4) → (0, 6) → (0, 2)
	[0, 3]	(0, 3) → (0, 1) → (0, 5) → (0, 4) → (0, 6) → (0, 2) → (0, 3)
*M*6:	[0, 1]	(0, 1) → (0, 6) → (0, 1)
	[0, 2]	(0, 2) → (0, 5) → (0, 2)
	[0, 3]	(0, 3) → (0, 4) → (0, 3)

form the foundation interval for the second sonority of the series, upon which is again superimposed an interval three times its size, namely the interval 9, denoted by the integer notation 4..6; this process continues. Thus the foundation interval of each sonority in the series can be thought of as the product of an M3 operation on the foundation interval of the

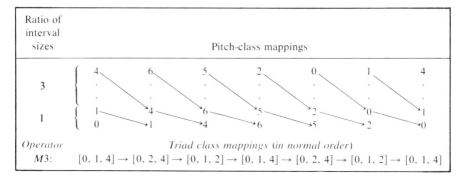

FIGURE 3.4. Randall's Series.

ETS 7

FIGURE 3.5. Variation on a thing by JKR. (Copyright © 1980 by Carlton Gamer.)

Notes on the score

1. Lines and spaces here do not denote the scale degrees of the traditional diatonic "white-key" subcollection of ETS 12. Rather they denote the scale degrees of ETS 7, with pitch class "C" = 0, "D" = 1, "E" = 2, . . ., "B" = 6 of that system.

2. A hollow dot (○) adds $\frac{1}{4}$ to the durational value of the note or rest that precedes it. A dot following a right bracket (]) adds $\frac{1}{2}$ to the durational value of the dotted note or rest that precedes the bracket.

3. "I_1", "I_2", and "I_3" refer to any three matched instruments capable of performing the designated pitches within the system. My own realization of this piece was on the IBM 360/91 Computer and at the Winham Laboratory of the Princeton University Department of Music, with the programming assistance of Richard Cann. In this realization, the instrumental spectra were designed in such a way that the frequencies of the "partials" of a given tone are not integral multiples of its fundamental frequency, as in the classical timbral model, but are based instead on the frequency ratios of the pitch classes of ETS 7, as shown in Table 3.4.

preceding sonority. Beneath the pitch-class mappings are shown the mappings of the prime forms of the sonorities in the series.

Nothing comparable to Randall's series can be found in ETS 12, of course, since in that system, as we have already noted, no interval under multiplication has a period greater than 2. Thus we see in this model, or in others that might be similarly derived, a structure hitherto unavailable for compositional realization.

The piece itself is given as Figure 3.5.

ETSs and Just Intonation

I shall now return to the problem of just intonation to which I referred in the introduction.

The three ETSs with which, for illustrative purposes, I have been primarily dealing up to this point—ETS 7, ETS 11, and ETS 13—belong to a large family of ETSs sometimes termed *inharmonic;* that is, the frequency ratios of the pitches within these systems deviate significantly from the just frequency ratios of the partials of the harmonic series.

The deviations can be seen in Table 3.4, which shows the frequency ratios (denoted FR) of the scale degrees in ETS 7, ETS 11, and ETS 13 as these compare to ETS 12 and to certain just ratios chosen from among the lower partials of the harmonic series.

Now consider Table 3.5, which shows the frequency ratios of selected scale degrees of three other systems, ETS 19, ETS 31, and ETS 53, as these compare to ETS 12 and to the same just ratios as in Table 3.4. It can be seen that in each of these systems, and particularly in ETS 31 and ETS 53, the "fit" with the just ratios is generally a better one than is that of any of the systems discussed above.

Of these systems, ETS 31 deserves special mention. Not only do certain of its intervals show only slight deviations from the just ratios, but it offers some powerful combinational resources as well. As was pointed out on page 68, ETS 31 contains exactly 15 interval classes. A representative of each of these can be contained in any of five difference sets of cardinality 6; each difference set can generate a cyclic block design. (I have listed and discussed these difference sets, as well as discussing other properties of the system, in my earlier articles.)[16] ETS 31 therefore lends itself to compositional exploitation in a number of significant ways.

Because of their relative goodness of fit with the just ratios, ETS 19, ETS 31, ETS 53 and a number of other systems that share this attribute

16. Gamer, "Combinational Resources" and "Deep Scales."

TABLE 3.4
Frequency Ratios of ETS 7, ETS 11, ETS 13, ETS 12

7		11		13		12		
Degree	FR	Degree	FR	Degree	FR	Degree	FR	Just ratios
0	1	0	1	0	1	0	1	1/1 = 1
		1	1.0650	1	1.0548	1	1.0595	—
1	1.1040	2	1.1343	2	1.1125	2	1.1225	{10/9 = 1.1111, 9/8 = 1.1250
				3	1.1735			
2	1.2190	3	1.2081	4	1.2377	3	1.1892	6/5 = 1.2000
		4	1.2867			4	1.2600	5/4 = 1.2500
				5	1.3055			
3	1.3459	5	1.3703	6	1.3770	5	1.3348	4/3 = 1.3333
		6	1.4594			6	1.4142	—
4	1.4860			7	1.4524	7	1.4983	3/2 = 1.5000
		7	1.5544	8	1.5320			8/5 = 1.6000
				9	1.6159	8	1.5874	
5	1.6407	8	1.6555			9	1.6818	5/3 = 1.6667
				10	1.7044			
		9	1.7632			10	1.7818	{ 7/4 = 1.7500
6	1.8114			11	1.7938			{ 9/5 = 1.8000
		10	1.8779					
				12	1.8962	11	1.8877	15/8 = 1.8750
7(0)	2	11(0)	2	13(0)	2	12(0)	2	2/1 = 2

TABLE 3.5
Frequency Ratios of ETS 19, ETS 31, ETS 53, ETS 12

19		31		53		12		
Degree	FR	Degree	FR	Degree	FR	Degree	FR	Just ratios
0	1	0	1	0	1	0	1	1/1 = 1
3	1.1157	5	1.1183	9	1.1249	2	1.1225	{10/9 = 1.1111, 9/8 = 1.1250
5	1.2001	8	1.1958	14	1.2009	3	1.1892	6/5 = 1.2000
6	1.2447	10	1.2505	17	1.2490	4	1.2600	5/4 = 1.2500
8	1.3389	13	1.3373	22	1.3334	5	1.3348	4/3 = 1.3333
11	1.4983	18	1.4956	31	1.4999	7	1.4983	3/2 = 1.5000
13	1.6068	21	1.5993	36	1.6013	8	1.5874	8/5 = 1.6000
14	1.6665	23	1.6725	39	1.6654	9	1.6818	5/3 = 1.6667
16	1.7927	25	1.7489	43	1.7548	10	1.7818	{ 7/4 = 1.7500, 9/5 = 1.8000
17	1.8593	28	1.8702	48	1.8734	11	1.8877	15/8 = 1.8750
19(0)	2	31(0)	2	53(0)	2	12(0)	2	2/1 = 2

have been emphasized in the literature to the virtual exclusion of the so-called "inharmonic" systems. The latter have generally been regarded as devoid of musical value.[17]

While sharing the conviction that goodness of fit is indeed an important criterion in the determination of the musical value of an ETS, I do not believe that its absence warrants the exclusion of an ETS from consideration. At best, any ETS is a compromise with the harmonic purity of a proportional tuning system based on the just ratios. Even the best fit can never be more than an approximation, however close, of those ratios. From this standpoint, then, even the "best" ETS must be regarded as relatively inharmonic; the difference between such a system and the more radically inharmonic systems, such as ETS 7, ETS 11, and ETS 13, is one of degree.

Given its relative inharmonicity, the reason for choosing an ETS rather than a proportional system for compositional purposes is the same as the reason for the adoption during the past two centuries of ETS 12 in lieu of its historical predecessors, namely the availability in any ETS of certain kinds of operations upon collections (especially that of transposition) and hence the possibility of certain kinds of tonal architecture.

For many listeners in the twentieth century, ETS 12, which is itself a relatively inharmonic system—though less radically so than ETS 7, ETS 11, or ETS 13—has become the "natural language" for the making of music. ETS 19, ETS 31, ETS 53, and the other less radically inharmonic systems whose goodness of fit with the just ratios is comparable to that of ETS 12 may well be heard by such listeners as "dialects" of ETS 12. The pitches of many scale degrees in these systems may be heard as "sounding in the cracks" of ETS 12.

For the composer employing one of these relatively well-fitting ETSs, this way of hearing it on the listener's part could prove either advantageous or problematic: advantageous in that ETS 12 might serve the listener as a comfortable frame of reference; problematic in that structures unique to the system being employed might not be heard as characteristic of that system but interpreted instead as variants of structures in ETS 12.

It is precisely in response to this last problem that the more radically inharmonic ETSs, like those described in this article, recommend themselves to our attention. These are systems less likely to be heard as "dialects" than as new languages. There are those who feel that these languages are so inherently discordant as to lie beyond the pale of musical acceptability. My own conviction as a composer is that the perception of

---

17. For an opposing point of view, see Ivor Darreg, "New Moods," Part II, *Interval: A Microtonal Newsletter* 1, no. 2 (1978): 7–8.

concord or discord can be made context-dependent and that inharmonicity per se, while it may challenge the composer's ingenuity, need not prevent the establishment of contextual norms governing such perception. Moreover, I feel that the revelation within a composition of such structures as have been described in this chapter, regardless of the degree of inharmonicity of the ETS itself, can be a thing of beauty.

It has been my intention in what I have written, then, to introduce some alternative criteria for determining the musical value of various ETSs. I do so without discounting the traditional criteria; rather, it is my hope that composers and their listeners might not only be made aware of the beneficial properties of ETSs hitherto neglected in the literature, but, moreover, might find, within the total universe of structures afforded by ETSs of every kind, material for the creation of new and exciting musical worlds.

4

Allan R. Keiler

MUSIC AS METALANGUAGE:
RAMEAU'S FUNDAMENTAL BASS

I

Fredric Jameson, in his book *The Prison-House of Language,* has remarked that "the history of thought is the history of its models. Classical
mechanics, the organism, natural selection, the atomic nucleus or electronic field, the computer: such are some of the objects or systems which,
first used to organize our understanding of the natural world, have then
been called upon to illuminate human reality."[1] In the history of music
theory it would not be difficult to show such a pattern of change: the principle of unity residing in the mathematical properties of the vibrating body
in the time of Rameau; language, especially discourse, as a model in discussions of the periodic form of phrase structure in the classical period; or
the organic model, associated with sources as different as Goethe and
Hegel, in the harmonic theories of Schenker and Hauptmann in the nineteenth century.

Several corollary ideas are bound up with Jameson's observation. One
is that a new awareness or intuition about how questions are to be formulated or problems solved can very often occur, sometimes over long periods of time, without the development or discovery having taken place of
an appropriate model or theoretical language in which to organize and
clarify new perceptions. This phenomenon is certainly a part of what
Thomas Kuhn has called the preparadigm period of research, a period in
which thinking has already shifted conclusively but before the transfor-

1. Fredric Jameson, *The Prison-House of Language* (Princeton: Princeton University
Press, 1972), p. v.

MUSIC THEORY: SPECIAL TOPICS

mation of some useful metaphor, for example, the organic metaphor of the nineteenth century, into a theoretical language in which appropriate generalizations can be made explicit. The period preceding that of Rameau's *Traité de l'harmonie* is surely one such period, during which a growing awareness of the triadic principle and of the syntax of harmonic progression could not yet be translated into an available analytic language. And although I would not be the first to have pointed out that theory follows practice, I am emphasizing the need to consider very carefully one determinant of this process of theoretical maturing: how a new theoretical language is created and applied to the solving of analytic problems. And a corollary idea to this is that an analytic language can very often be pressed into the service of representing new attitudes and novel solutions to problems for which the language was never intended. Both situations, the absence of an appropriate or sufficiently developed theoretical model in which to formalize new attitudes to the problem-solving activity of music theory, and the use of analytic tools that are either intrinsically not suitable, or not clarified sufficiently by theorists in new analytic contexts, are not uncommon and will add to the strain of interpretation in the history of music theory.

The concept of the fundamental bass, one of the central ideas in the theories of Rameau, will serve as the basis for a discussion and application of the preliminary ideas outlined above.[2] The fundamental bass of Rameau is generally understood to be that fictitious (or analytic) bass line that consists of the roots of the chords of a succession of harmonies, an analytic device that Rameau used to represent the root movement of chords abstracted from the particular inversions that actually occur in any sequence of harmonies. But this definition is a misleading oversimplification, which suggests neither the much broader range of uses of the fundamental bass nor the contradictions it sometimes occasioned in Rameau's work and the controversy it generated among the generation of theorists that followed Rameau.

Rameau himself intended the fundamental bass as an analytic representation of the root progression of chords: "The fundamental bass is given only to show the progression of harmonies; it is not intended to be heard below the other parts."[3] But in the earlier treatises, especially the *Traité*

---

2. Although the relationship of the fundamental bass to the mathematical and physical properties of sound was of primary importance to Rameau, I do not discuss this aspect of Rameau's concept in this paper. It seems to me that this connection too often detracts from the problem of the nature of the analytic solutions proposed by Rameau, even though it is clear that the natural basis of Rameau's theories usually entails unfortunate constraints on the problem-solving alternatives available to him.

3. "La Basse fondamentale n'est donnée que pour connoître l'Harmonie et ses routes, nullement pour être entendue au-dessous des autres parties." Jean-Philippe Rameau, *Gén-*

de l'harmonie, Rameau is not always perfectly clear, certainly not in practice, about the distinction between basso continuo and fundamental bass,
the former the actual musical bass line, and the latter a fictitious bass used
to show the one-to-many relationship between root position chord and
derived inversions. Hans Pischner, in his important study *Die Harmonielehre Jean-Philippe Rameaus,* touches on this question when he argues
that "the fundamental bass decisively controls the proper harmonization
of a melody. It also determines the basso continuo. In essence, in Rameau's opinion, the true basso continuo ought to be the same as the fundamental bass."[4] This is very much a paraphrase of Rameau, who argues,
in the passage that begins the forty-first chapter of Book III ("Principles
of Composition") of the *Traité,* "How to compose a Basso Continuo
below a Treble": "The true basso continuo ought to be the fundamental.
It is customary, however, to distinguish from the fundamental that part
that is dictated by good taste and which makes allowances for the
progressions of the other parts written above it, by calling this part the
continuo."[5]

More important than Rameau's observation that the basso continuo
need not necessarily be distinct from the fundamental bass is his claim,
developed in chapters 40 and 41 of Part III, that the basso continuo is actually transformed from an already existing fundamental bass, which in
some sense is composed before the basso continuo. The latter, in other
words, may be derived from the fundamental bass in the interest, for example, of good taste, variety, or the avoidance of closure. Rameau's discussion of the relationship between basso continuo and fundamental bass
in these chapters is not very different from any present-day pedagogical
practice that instructs the student to work out a bass line for a piece (or
example) that is limited to harmonies in root progression, so as to insure
the syntactical correctness of the choice of harmonies; he may then alter
his first attempt (which is, in fact, Rameau's fundamental bass) by choosing chord inversions in order to achieve a bass line with more conjunct
motion, more direction, and less repetition of fifth relationships. In the
process, the original bass line is clearly understood as a possible musical
part (indeed, it plays that role for a time) and therefore assumes the role of

ération harmonique (1737), p. 190. Trans. mine. Rameau's theoretical writings have been
published by the American Institute of Musicology, edited by Erwin R. Jacobi, in six vol-
umes (1967–72). The *Génération* is vol. 3, the *Traité de l'harmonie* is vol. 1. See also Joan
Ferris, "The Evolution of Rameau's Harmonic Theories," *Journal of Music Theory* 3
(1959), p. 240.

4. Hans Pischner, *Die Harmonielehre Jean-Philippe Rameaus* (Leipzig: Breitkopf and
Härtel, 1967), p. 113. Trans. mine.

5. Jean-Philippe Rameau, *Treatise on Harmony,* trans., with an Introduction and Notes,
Philip Gossett (New York: Dover, 1971), p. 341.

a simple precompositional plan with respect to the final bass line. Once the process is completed, the original bass can be thought of as an analytic representation in the sense that it generalizes: Any number of different basso continuo parts can be seen as possible derivations of the same sequence of harmonic relationships represented by the fundamental bass. It is because of these practical concerns of composition, so important to Rameau as a part of his theoretical work, that the fundamental bass and basso continuo could both be treated as musical parts, at least for some stage of the process of musical composition.

It would not be surprising, therefore, to see this lack of clarity concerning the exclusive functions of basso continuo and fundamental bass reflected in Rameau's analytic decisions. Sometimes Rameau is quite explicit about the status of the fundamental bass as one of the possible musical parts of an example. Consider, for example, what he says about the perfect cadence (Figure 4.1):

> It is from Ex. II.1, then, that we should derive all the different methods of using the perfect cadence, whether in two, three, four, or five parts. We choose as many parts as we wish to use together, and place them in any desired order. Those parts found above may be placed below, etc. Only the fundamental bass cannot naturally change its position, although even it is free

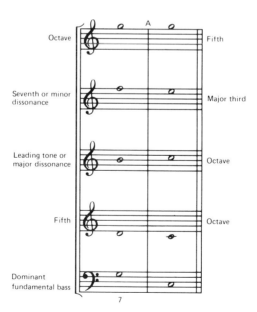

FIGURE 4.1. Rameau's analysis of the perfect cadence.

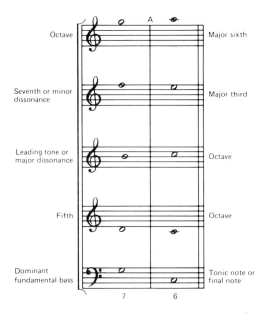

FIGURE 4.2. Rameau's analysis of the deceptive cadence.

from constraint as long as good taste guides us. To avoid a perfect conclusion, it may be placed in an upper part, while the bass [*continuo*] proceeds diatonically.[6]

Or take Rameau's analysis of the deceptive cadence (Figure 4.2) about which he argues: "If parts A of Ex. II.5 are then placed below the fundamental bass, we shall simply find a seventh chord and a perfect chord, in accordance with our initial proposition. The deceptive cadence is most often used in this manner"; and "Remember that the fundamental bass may be used in the treble only when good taste permits and that the deceptive cadence is perceived only when the fifth is transposed to the sixth. . . ."[7] I will come back to these examples later. But it is already clear from examples such as these that the fundamental bass for Rameau is not entirely without significance as a (possible or potential) musical part, in addition to its status as a fictitious or purely analytic representation of the underlying root progression of chords.

As for the controversy and misunderstandings that were occasioned by Rameau's fundamental bass during the generation of theorists that fol-

6. Ibid., p. 70.
7. Ibid., p. 73.

FIGURE 4.3. An example of the interpolated bass in Rameau.

lowed Rameau, let us begin by considering Marpurg's view of the conflict that surrounded the application of the fundamental bass.

> Since Kirnberger's fundamental bass mainly depends upon the extractor's himself composing and substituting his personal whims for the thoughts of the composer, instead of breaking down the existing tonal fabric and reducing the given construction to its simple elements, so might Kirnberger's fundamental bass be termed not a true fundamental bass, but an *interpolated bass*.[8]

Figure 4.3 is an example of the so-called interpolated bass, which was not an invention of Kirnberger, but is a procedure that Rameau himself made use of in all of the treatises. Rameau, in other words, incorporates into his fundamental bass a number of procedures that depart from the view that the fundamental bass adheres strictly to the musical surface by containing only the root of those chords that actually occur in the musical example. In Figure 4.3 the fundamental bass appears to contain, or at least make reference to more harmonic material (the D at letter B) than is actually present in the given sequence of chords. In Figure 4.4 the procedure in the fundamental bass is less radical: The same chord is analyzed differently and provided with two different notes in the fundamental bass (letters A and B). It is procedures like these, taken over by Kirnberger, that prompted such admonitions by Marpurg as the following: "The funda-

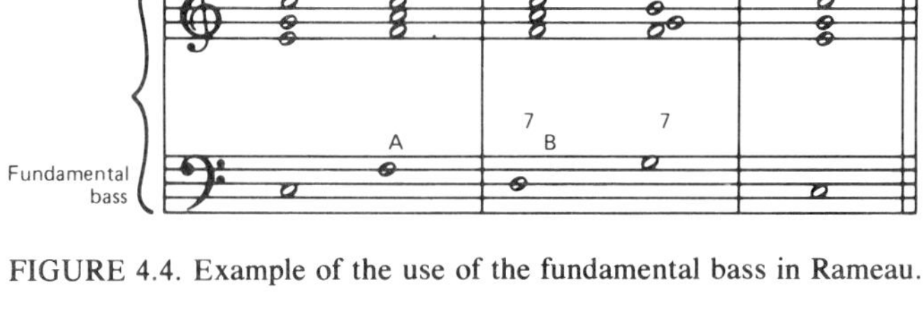

FIGURE 4.4. Example of the use of the fundamental bass in Rameau.

8. Trans. in Cecil Powell Grant, "The Real Relationship between Kirnberger's and Rameau's Concept of the Fundamental Bass," *Journal of Music Theory* 21 (1977), p. 334.

FIGURE 4.5. Example of the interpolated bass in Kirnberger.

mental bass should not say what the composer could have said had he so wished, but rather what he actually did say."[9] Marpurg, who tries to pass himself off as more empirical, considers that Kirnberger's use of the fundamental bass often departs from what was originally intended by Rameau.

Kirnberger did extend the use of Rameau's fundamental bass to analytic contexts where the fundamental bass is not restricted to representing the root of those chords actually occurring in the musical surface and which are not, in fact, discussed by Rameau. Consider Figure 4.5, where the sequence A B of the fundamental bass is used in a context of harmonic conflation. The seventh of the first dominant chord does not resolve properly to E, but moves directly to the third of the next dominant seventh chord; only the soprano of the second chord represents any overt resolution of the first chord. Again this kind of example might suggest that the fundamental bass, in implying the presence of chords that do not exist in the musical surface, actually distorts the musical example. And this kind of criticism is still echoed in present-day writers. Mekeel, for example, has argued that "the fundamental bass, as originally conceived by Rameau, cannot contain more than is contained in the original example."[10] Here again is the implication that one ought not to substitute one's own amplified or recomposed version, in the form of a fundamental bass, of what is already in the musical surface itself.

To understand the basis of these different views about the fundamental bass, we need to draw an analogy with language.[11] Consider first the sen-

9. Trans. in Joyce Mekeel, "The Harmonic Theories of Kirnberger and Marpurg," *Journal of Music Theory* 4 (1960), p. 186.

10. Ibid., p. 184.

11. I have discussed the relationship of language to music in several articles that the reader may find useful in relation to some of the discussion in this paper: "Bernstein's *The Unanswered Question* and the Problem of Musical Competence," *The Musical Quarterly* 64 (1978), pp. 195–222; "The Syntax of Prolongation," *In Theory Only* 3 (1977), pp. 3–27; "Two Views of Musical Semiotics," in *The Sign in Word and Language*, ed. Wendy Steiner (Austin: University of Texas Press, in press).

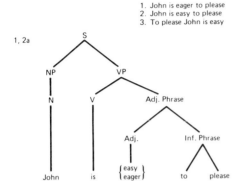
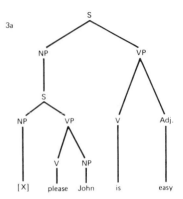

FIGURE 4.6. Phrase structure analysis of English sentence patterns.

tences in Figure 4.6. The first sentence, if broken down hierarchically into constituents, would be described by the diagram in 1a, in which each word is related to its immediate constituent, and similarly each group of words, and that information is made explicit by a hierarchical division of syntactic classes and the constituents that expand each class. The tree diagram associated with these sentences thus contains two kinds of syntactic information: (*a*) abstract syntactic classes, such as NP (noun phrase), VP (verb phrase), etc., which make explicit the principal categories of syntactic expansion, and (*b*) immediate constituent relationships, which define the degree to which the words in a sentence modify or relate to each other.

Now even though the syntactic structures of sentences 1 and 2 are different in important ways, the second sentence would also have to be broken up into immediate constituents in the same way. The same tree diagram thus serves to indicate that nothing in the surface arrangement of words distinguishes the syntactic form of the first two sentences. But now consider their underlying differences. In *John is easy to please, John* has to be understood as the object, not subject, of *please*, which is not true of 1, but cannot be understood as the subject of the infinitive, which **is** true for 1. However, 2 and 3 are related in important ways. They have the same meaning and are clearly alternate forms of the same syntactic structure. *To please John is easy*, in fact, is explicit in its surface form in just the ways that *John is easy to please* is not. In the former, *John* actually occurs in the object position following the infinitive, and the surface subject of the sentence is the infinitive phrase, and not *John*. One would then argue that if 3a represents the syntactic constituent structure of 3, then it must underlie 2 as well. *To please John is easy,* in other words, is a more explicit form of the same syntactic pattern than *John is easy to please.* By explicit I mean that its surface form can be more directly related to the underlying syntactic representation. Now the relationship between the two sentences (2 and 3) that concerns us here could be called one of paraphrase. Let us further distinguish between semantic and syntactic paraphrase. As an example of the former, the sentence *A bachelor is an unmarried man* can be said to paraphrase or gloss the lexical item *bachelor* in the sentence *John is a bachelor.* The function of *A bachelor is an unmarried man* is not referential but metalinguistic; that is, its primary communicative function is to point out some aspect of the language code. Sentence 3, however, could be called a syntactic paraphrase of 2—its surface form is a more explicit version of 2. *To please John is easy,* then, is used referentially when it is offered as a claim or a response to something about the real world, but can also function metalinguistically when it is offered as a paraphrase of 2. In other words, at least in specific cases, language is both the subject of inquiry and the result of that same activity. And although not every sentence can or need have this dual semiotic function, all sentences that are used metalinguistically must necessarily be ordinary language. The same linguistic code generates both classes of sentences.

We can now consider Rameau's fundamental bass from the same perspective and hope to make some sense of the divergent attitudes toward it that I have pointed out. The first point, however obvious it may seem, has important implications: It is that the notational vocabulary of the fundamental bass is taken over entirely from the older basso continuo and thus makes use of pitch notation on a staff and figured-bass numerals. Indeed, a fundamental bass, taken away from its association with a basso continuo indicated as the next higher musical part, is no different in appearance from a basso continuo. The difference in collection between the two, that is, in the class of possible examples that make up each, is only a matter of divergence—basso continuos are more divergent in character than are fundamental basses. Consider the simplest possible situation, a musical example whose chords happen to be entirely in root position. The bass would then, presumably, have to be understood in two different ways: as a musical part, hence something intended by the composer and part of the corpus that defines the subject of inquiry, and, at the same time, as the result of analysis, that is, an analytic statement about harmonic progression—the musical substance has been turned into a metalinguistic representation of harmonic structure. Both basso continuo and fundamental bass are constrained by the same rules of harmonic syntax. As for those situations in which the fundamental bass would not be the same as the basso continuo, Rameau considers that the fundamental bass is simply transformed into the basso continuo, in the interest, for example, of avoiding undesirable harmonic closure, of giving a greater tension to the melodic line, etc. He says as much when he argues that:

> We often depart from the natural progression of the bass so as to avoid the frequent conclusions which the bass makes us feel when it follows its most perfect progression. We do this by drawing a note from each chord forming the conclusion and placing them in the bass instead of the most natural note. By this means we can maintain that suspension in melody and harmony which the subject demands, for the absolute conclusion is suitable only when the meaning is concluded. The following chapter will clarify this.[12]

This comes at the end of the chapter ''On How to Compose a Fundamental Bass Below a Treble.''[13] The following chapter, the forty-first, begins with the assertion: ''The true basso continuo ought to be the fundamental,'' which I quoted earlier; the force of Rameau's assertion is now clear. Rameau's pedagogical approach in Book III of the *Traité* is premised on the possibility of considering the fundamental bass both as a (temporary) musical bass line and as a metalinguistic analytic statement about music. As metalanguage, the fundamental bass has the character of paraphrase, representing musically the most explicit, prototypical form that underlies the musical example being analyzed.

II

Briefly to recapitulate the essential points, the fundamental bass of Rameau makes use of musical notation as analytic vocabulary for analytic statements **about** music. The fundamental bass must thus conform to musical as well as analytic constraints. The fundamental bass, in other words, must already exist as a possible musical bass within the general musical style, since it is the **musical** notation available within the musical corpus that is transformed in function to serve as **analytic** notation. It is not surprising, but certainly unusual, that Rameau devotes an entire chapter of the *Traité* to the problem of **composing** a fundamental bass. One does not, in the normal sense, **compose** analytic statements about music, but rather represents structural facts about music by means of analytic vocabulary. Musical notation, however, as we have seen, can be made to serve as analytic notation by representing the most explicit musical version of a musical surface. Consider again Figures 4.3 and 4.4. The most

12. Rameau, *Treatise*, Gossett trans. pp. 340–41.
13. Ibid., pp. 331–41.

FIGURE 4.7. Example of Rameau's fundamental bass.

explicit musical surface that conforms to the same harmonic progression as those of Figures 4.3 and 4.4 is given in Figure 4.7, where the supertonic fundamental bass, at letter A, is actually present in the musical surface. I think it is plausible to suggest that, for Rameau, all of these examples were different surface realizations of the same basic harmonic progression; the solution in terms of a fundamental bass is to assign the most explicit musical root-position bass line (the fundamental bass), the one that, in fact, underlies only Figure 4.7 in a directly isomorphic way, to all three examples. The analytic function of the fundamental bass in relation to Figures 4.3 and 4.4 is, then, one of musical paraphrase in the specific sense that I have discussed above. That language and music are both capable of functioning analytically *about* language and music results from fundamental properties that both share. One such property is that the structures of natural languages and tonal music (perhaps all musical systems) are constrained by general syntactical properties which, by iterative application, create an infinitely large class of possible examples. It will always be the case, therefore, that instances in both domains (language as well as music) can always be considered derived or transformed from more basic and prototypical (or less complex or elaborated) instances. This relation is particularly true of certain syntactical aspects of sentence structure and of harmonic prolongation. Another property that both share is derivational operations, which create surface forms that are related in irregular, elliptical, or otherwise transformed ways to more general underlying forms. In the case of the former, metalinguistic statements will tend to be reductive (i.e., will have the form of reductions); in the case of the latter, they will tend to have the property of paraphrase (i.e., will be more explicit).

Note finally that very often an analytic solution in terms of the fundamental bass must also entail a (unnecessarily imposed) musical solution. In Figure 4.3, for example, since Rameau must indicate that the same chord fulfills two harmonic functions, and this must be represented analytically with two fundamental bass notes, a musical solution is required with respect to duration and, by implication, harmonic rhythm, decisions that should be quite beside the point when dealing with abstract harmonic relations.[14] One is forced, in other words, to make musical decisions about the form of the fundamental bass in addition to analytic decisions, and the former are forced upon the analyst because of the status of musical notation functioning as metalanguage. It is often not possible to separate the analytic decisions from (what ought to be unnecessary) musical decisions. One result of this is that many uses of the fundamental bass of Rameau will appear as unwarranted musical recompositions, distorting or conflicting with the actual musical surface. The musical nature of the fundamental bass in these cases is not being separated from the metalinguistic (analytic) function of the musical notation. This is certainly the basis of the criticisms of Marpurg against Kirnberger, and in general of those critics of Rameau who find interpolated basses, for example, as unmotivated departures from the examples being analyzed. In Figure 4.3 or examples like that of Figure 4.8, Rameau simply assigns a separate fundamental bass note to each of the harmonic functions realized in these examples as only a single chord on the musical surface. The fundamental bass of Figure 4.3, in other words, should be read in the following way: The triad in the first half of the second measure has both the function of relating to the preceding tonic as part of a plagal relation, and to the following chord as a dominant preparation chord (for Rameau the supertonic fundamental bass rep-

FIGURE 4.8. Example of the interpolated bass in Rameau.

14. Too much is made of the idea that Rameau's primary concern in these examples was to avoid at all costs fundamental bass progressions by step. His treatises do not suggest this absolute stricture, and, indeed, in the later ones, step progressions are to be found in the fundamental bass. In addition, as I will argue later, although many of Rameau's analytic solutions resulted in this avoidance of step progressions, he was more concerned with a theory of explicit chord function. All of this is particularly clear in Rameau's analysis of the deceptive cadence, which is discussed below.

resents analytically a subdominant chord, IV and II$_5^6$ or II^7, that progresses necessarily to the dominant seventh).

The preceding discussion raises a general point about the use of musical metalanguage for the purpose of analysis. Since any metalinguistic statement, for example Rameau's fundamental bass, will at the same time be a perfectly good example of the object of inquiry, one must derive analytic notation from musical notation by explicit conventions or rules on how to read musical notation analytically. Metalinguistic statements in music are as open to the same wide variety of interpretation, reaction, and perceptual viewpoints as any other music. The interpretation of musical notation as analytic notation, therefore, is not unlike that of any symbology: Conventions need to be established, within some explicit theoretical framework, that determine the analytic significance of such notation as the language in which general and often very abstract claims can be made about the musical surface.

Notice that if we changed from the metalinguistic fundamental bass of Rameau to the tree notation used above to describe the constituent analysis of sentences, the musical surfaces of Figures 4.3, 4.4, and 4.8 would all have the same harmonic structure, represented in Figure 4.9. The constituent structure of the chords of these examples is indicated as branching relations and in terms of syntactic categories of expansion and their hierarchical relationships (TP = tonic prolongation, TC = tonic completion, DP = dominant prolongation, D = dominant, S = subdominant, T = tonic). The subdominant triad is thus defined as entering into two harmonic relationships: It is attached as a branch to two different harmonic categories, and is thus an immediate constituent of the preceding tonic triad and of the following dominant seventh chord. In Figure 4.3, the

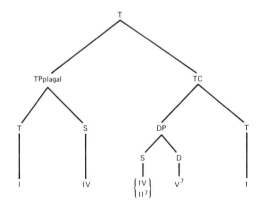

FIGURE 4.9. Syntactical analysis of harmonic constituents.

two subdominant branches are realized, by virtue of shared pitch content, as the same chord on the musical surface. It is important to emphasize here that no musical decision is forced upon the analyst in terms of notational vocabulary, since abstract harmonic relationships are not represented metalinguistically by musical notation.

We must now ask how the interpretation of the fundamental bass discussed here is reflected in the actual activity of problem solving, how the dual nature of the fundamental bass helps us to make sense not only of its application in the theories of Rameau, but of its reception by later theorists. Rameau's analysis of the deceptive cadence in the *Traité* (see Figure 4.2) will illustrate many of the points I have been making. Notice first that, in order to derive the deceptive cadence from the more prototypical perfect cadence, Rameau indicates the prescribed fifth relationship in the fundamental bass.[15] He then must revert back to the Baroque principle of the basso continuo when he adds the 6 below the tonic note. This 6 has nothing to do with chord inversion (indeed, figures, especially inversion figures, ought not to be in the fundamental bass at all); it simply indicates that the 5 must be changed to 6 in order to specify properly the pitch (interval) content in the upper parts. Moreover, it is not correct to claim, as some have, that with this analysis Rameau argues that the deceptive cadence occurs predominantly in first inversion. We need Rameau's own commentary on this example now:

> If these examples [Figure 4.2] are compared with those of the perfect cadence [Ex. II.1], the only difference we shall find is that here the fifth ascends to the sixth in the parts marked A. If parts A of Ex. II.5 [Figure 4.2] are then placed below the fundamental bass, we shall simply find a seventh chord and a perfect, in accordance with our initial proposition. The deceptive cadence is most often used in this manner. . . . Remember that the fundamental bass may be used in the treble only when good taste permits and that the deceptive cadence is perceived only when the fifth is transposed to the sixth; i.e., when the sixth takes the place of the fifth found in the perfect chord which terminates the perfect cadence. All other parts remain the same in both cadences. Observe that when part A is used as the bass, it is preferable to place the octave of the third in the chord, rather than the octave of the bass. This is because the third implies the true fundamental sound, whose replicate cannot be displeasing.[16]

The complex nature of the fundamental bass is apparent from this analysis. From this example, we can generalize about the whole analytic pro-

15. Another reason that Rameau indicates a fundamental fifth progression for the deceptive cadence is his desire to define chord function in terms of the intrinsic property of each scale degree chord to progress in a determined way. For Rameau the prototypical function of the dominant chord is to progress to the tonic.

16. Rameau, *Treatise,* Gossett trans., p. 73.

cess, not atypical in the treatises of Rameau. The fundamental bass begins life as a musical part, so that the contrast between the fundamental bass and the basso continuo is not yet significant. It then assumes additionally its analytic (i.e., metalinguistic) function, that of an underlying representation, from which generalizations can be made about chord inversion, dissonance treatment, and harmonic progression. At the end of this rule-ordered stage, that is, postanalytically, the status of the fundamental bass must be reclarified, and Rameau, as I have already indicated, deals with the fundamental bass in more than a single way. Most important, of course, is its status as a hypothetical bass line, functioning analytically by virtue of its metalinguistic character. But in many cases Rameau characterizes it as a possible upper part when another part takes its place, as in the above example. This, according to Rameau, is determined by conditions of taste and stylistic appropriateness. Or, finally, it is (usually gradually) transformed into a basso continuo by retaining its position as the lowest sounding part. This transformational process tends, of course, to occur in the context of the more practical concerns of composition. This complex of interrelated stages is possible only as a result of the semiotic duality of music as metalanguage. This chameleon-like aspect of the fundamental bass, as perhaps we should expect, sometimes becomes unmanageable for Rameau. Consider for a moment longer Rameau's analysis of the deceptive cadence. In order to account for the doubled third of the final chord of the deceptive cadence, Rameau must appeal to the basso continuo part (i.e., A) as the lowest part from which to calculate intervals, rather than the fundamental bass, since the latter, which included the third of the chord, has by this stage in the process either been deleted or exchanged with the future basso continuo as an inner part. Rameau, in other words, in order to deal correctly with the facts of the musical surface, must contradict himself on a fundamental point, that of using his hypothetical fundamental bass as the basis for interval calculation, doubling, etc. It is not surprising that Rameau, in the later treatises, abandons the distinction between fundamental bass and basso continuo in this example, and identifies part A as the fundamental bass.

As a final example, let us consider briefly the problem of the *double emploi*. Simplified somewhat, there are several stages leading up to the *double emploi*, the final stage of which is given in Figure 4.10.[17] And this problem can be considered only in the context of Rameau's theory of chord function. About the latter we can, unfortunately, say even less here. The essential point, however, is that for Rameau the syntax of harmonic progression is defined for the most part as a function of scale-de-

17. See Matthew Shirlaw, *The Theory of Harmony* (London: Novello, 1917), pp. 191–197, from which this figure is drawn.

FIGURE 4.10. Rameau's analysis of the *double emploi* in the *Génération harmonique*.

gree progression and appropriate dissonance. The perfect cadence represents the model for Rameau's idea of chord function because—and this is the most important issue—the immediate constituent relationship between seventh chord and perfect chord can be defined both explicitly and exhaustively by the musical surface: The root of the dominant chord progresses by fifth to its chord of resolution, and the dissonance, prepared properly, resolves to the third of the tonic chord. Rameau believed, in other words, that the progression of a chord to its constituent chord of resolution is due to some intrinsic property of that chord that conditions its progress in a deterministic way. Scale degree and dissonance resolution determine and therefore define chord function as a necessary relationship between satellite chord and chord of resolution. Rameau is then prepared to add to the musical surface those, for him, necessary overt musical manifestations of what are actually abstract relationships of harmonic succession. The liberal addition to the fundamental bass of the dissonance of the seventh, for example, to a satellite chord progressing by fifth, whether or not the dissonance actually occurs in the musical surface, must be considered a departure analytically from the use of figured bass numerals. In these examples, Rameau is attempting to represent **potential attributes** of chords that, in the most prototypical cases, are actually present in the musical surface and are part of the surface definition of the function of a certain class of chords. It is, in other words, an attempt to define the minimally unambiguous surface implementation of a syntactical constituent relationship. This is another example of the fact that the fundamental bass, because of its prototypical nature as metalanguage, has a more explicit character in many cases than the musical surface. Again, there is no question of distortion, or of an unempirical attitude toward the musical facts, but rather an attempt to characterize, with the use of musical metalanguage, those musical surfaces that are in some sense distortions of underlying regularities, regularities which in other examples are realized in a more straightforward and isomorphic manner on the musical surface.

Rameau's views about chord function, then, are premised on an isomorphic relationship between surface form and chord function. Rameau, of course, slowly came to associate this function with scale degree, and he had the greatest problems with the subdominant or fourth scale degree, because the same pitch collection could progress both to the tonic as well as to the dominant. He characterized the subdominant as a relationship that necessarily progresses to the tonic, and the supertonic, to the dominant. Those instances of a IV chord progressing to the dominant were interpreted as having a supertonic fundamental bass so that progression to the dominant could be generalized by the same notational device. Figure 4.4 is an example of this, in which the same triad (at B) is interpreted differently than it is at A, i.e., when it moves to the dominant. Too much is made about the avoidance of fundamental bass progressions that ascend by step in these contexts. The primary importance of examples like 3 and 4 pertains to their notationally unambiguous representation of chord function, and this Rameau was able to accomplish by the paraphrase device of a more explicit fundamental bass. Is this not supported by Rameau himself when, describing the situation in Figure 4.3, he comments: "We remarked in the preceding book that, whenever it is permissible to have the fundamental bass ascend a tone or a semitone, the progression of a third and a fourth is always implied."[18] In other words, for Rameau, the musical surface of Figure 4.3 is more elliptical than that in Figure 4.4: The subdominant triad occurs only a single 'time in the former, but the same fundamental bass will serve, for Rameau, as the explicit paraphrase of both examples. He thus assigns the more explicit fundamental bass to the reading of a chord whose surface form is not fully indicative of its harmonic function.[19] One might say that, restricted to the metalinguistic use of musical paraphrase as an analytic device, Rameau indicates in the fundamental bass what is required to differentiate both functions of the IV chord unambiguously. The same solution would be provided in those instances when the chord in question is a seventh chord (for Rameau, generally a II_5^6 chord).

The final version of the problem is the *double emploi* of Figure 4.10, where Rameau has explicitly recognized that the IV triad can indeed be ambiguous in terms of its surface form with respect to harmonic function. The fundamental bass note A at letter A indicates that the II progresses to the dominant. The subdominant fundamental bass C, in parentheses, is to be understood as potential, to be actualized only in the proper harmonic context, that is, before a tonic chord. This solution of the *double emploi* is, I think, a step backward for Rameau. In this case he devises, to use

18. Rameau, *Treatise*, Gossett trans., p. 234.

19. It should be clear from my discussions about the relation of Figures 4.3 and 4.4, and about Rameau's theory of chord function, that I cannot agree with those who argue that Rameau often willfully inserts a chord into the musical surface of such examples as those of Figures 4.3 and 4.4. But this is an easy mistake of interpretation to make until one understands the paraphrase nature of the fundamental bass.

some current terminology, an implication–realization solution by indicating both possible continuations of the same pitch collection (i.e., the seventh chord that would be realized at letter A of Figure 4.10) in the fundamental bass. He thus confuses the problem of structural ambiguity, which is an aspect of structural descriptions, with the problem of the perceiver, which is to revise hypothetical readings of the input as he receives more information. There is, moreover, a preferable interpretation of the *double emploi,* where the lower note of the fundamental bass makes explicit the plagal relation of the chord at A with the preceding tonic chord, and the A of the fundamental bass defines the dominant relationship of that chord with the following chord.

I would make the following remarks by way of conclusion. The source of Rameau's analytic vocabulary was figured-bass theory; the basso continuo as a musical part and the figures that indicated interval content in the other parts were converted by Rameau into the analytic language of the fundamental bass. Music, in other words, became the language of analysis for music, and both functions, music and metalanguage, were never really separated decisively from each other in the theories of Rameau. Since the primary metalinguistic function of music, just as in language, is paraphrase, and the essence of paraphrase is greater explicitness, many of Rameau's fundamental basses have this same property. It is not surprising, therefore, that many of Rameau's critics reacted to these as willful departures from the actual music, rather than as analytic statements about the musical surface. From our own perspective in the history of music theory, several important issues are raised by Rameau's treatises, issues that are still with us today. One is the question of whether music is an acceptable analytic language for music theory. Although it is customary to analyze, or at least to talk informally about one piece of music in terms of another, whether in the form of a reduction or paraphrase, it seems to me that one is very often left to extrapolate from one what is in the other. Another is the problem of how to relate the idiosyncratic musical surface to more constrained underlying structures. Rameau was the first theorist to be confronted, in the area of harmonic analysis, with the fact that the surface details of a piece often obscure the extent to which any piece conforms to the general musical language. Rameau's analytic language, limited to the metalinguistic function inherent in musical notation, forced him to represent abstract harmonic relationships in terms of explicit and precise musical paraphrases. What is most touching about Rameau, and what still appeals to us in his theoretical writings, is the magnitude of importance of the issues raised and the often primitive character of the solutions offered.

5

David Lewin

SOME INVESTIGATIONS INTO FOREGROUND RHYTHMIC AND METRIC PATTERNING

Introduction

The point of departure of this exploration will be a problem presented by Jeanne Bamberger.[1] A sound synthesizer had been programmed to generate a series of identical pulses, separated by successive durations of 2, 3, 4, and 5 time units, at a brisk tempo. The listener expected to respond to the stimulus as an ametric phenomenon, simply following the acoustic pattern symbolized by (5.1).

$$\text{(5.1)}$$

Instead, he was surprised to discover, in his own perception, a very strong metric response to the stimulus, which he "heard" as in (5.2).

$$\text{(5.2)}$$

Bamberger herself experienced the sense of (5.2) strongly, and I think it is reasonable to suppose that many listeners will be able to respond easily

---

1. Lecture in the panel, "Cognitive Approaches to Music Composition and Perception," First International Conference on Computer Music, Massachusetts Institute of Technology, October 29, 1976.

MUSIC THEORY: SPECIAL TOPICS

to the objective stimulus of (5.1), at a brisk tempo, in the mode of (5.2). I certainly can, though I do not feel obliged to.

I propose that this phenomenon requires and repays investigation. I do not mean this from the viewpoint of experimental psychology; I am not qualified to undertake such a study, and I am dubious as to what it could "prove" or "disprove," given such factors as musical education, received notation, etc. Rather, I propose to *assume* that it is possible (although not necessary) to have certain metric responses to the stimulus, and I shall investigate what numerical features of that stimulus might lead one to have such responses. I have in mind here, as the responses at issue, the hearing of special accents or marks on the third and fifth attacks [the bar lines of (5.2)], the hearing of the second duration as structurally equivalent to the first, the hearing of the first and second durations together as structurally equivalent to the third, and the hearing of the latter as structurally equivalent to the fourth.

One family of traditional explications would assert an innate two-ness or even four-ness about our reactions to musical rhythm; this innate response, whether philosophical or physiological, might force our perception of even such a simple stimulus as that of (5.1) into a suitable prescribed duple mold.[2] I cannot be satisfied by any such explanation here: There are many other simple foreground rhythmic patterns that I cannot hear as distortions of binary paradigms. Even passing over formidable grounds for disputing the theories themselves, then, I would be unwilling to invoke them as determinative in explicating the response of (5.2).

A second family of traditional explications would rely on the supposition that such binary processing, although not innate, is strongly conditioned into our particular culture; acculturation, functioning in the manner of an *Anschauung,* would then force our perception of (5.1) into the

---

2. The locus classicus for philosophical approaches of this sort can be found in the work of Moritz Hauptmann (*Die Natur der Harmonik und Metrik* [Leipzig: Breitkopf und Haertel, 1853]). Hauptmann bases his theory of meter on the Hegelian analysis and synthesis of dialectic tension between thetic and antithetic time spans. The approach, particularly as formulated in connection with the concept of *Entzweiung,* leads to a dialectic priority for duple and quadruple structures. The duple measure, in Hauptmann's metric theory, is formally analogous to the octave in his harmonic theory; the quadruple measure ought to come out as an analog to the harmonic triad. (Hauptmann's lack of dialectic skill leads to his confusing the latter situation.) Hugo Riemann continued the philosophical tradition with different formalism (*System der musikalischen Rhythmik und Metrik* [Leipzig: Breitkopf und Haertel, 1903]). Physiological theories of binary meter invoke the regular duple rhythm of one or more basic processes associated with the body: breathing, walking, coronary diastole and systole, etc. This notion goes back at least to the time of Franchinus Gafurius, who was already discussing such matters (*Practica musicae,* trans. Irwin Young [Madison, Milwaukee, and London: The University of Wisconsin Press, 1969], p. 69).

received mold of (5.2).[3] I would allow a certain weight to this argument, but I cannot accept it as determinant either. After all, I am listening now, not a century ago; whatever such conditioning may be latent within me, it does not seem so powerful as to interfere with my response to and composition of music quite incompatible with the rhythmic–metric *Anschauung* under discussion, music to which I have also become "conditioned," if that notion is to enter into consideration. Why, that is, should (5.1) itself, without preliminary processing, evoke a "Verdi" rather than a "Babbitt" complex of conditioned responses in my ear? (If anything, the physical circumstances surrounding the actual sound production should evoke the latter responses quite strongly.) For these reasons, I am reluctant to allow acculturation much force here, beyond perhaps the idea of organizing rhythm "metrically" itself.

Nor are the approaches of recent "stratification" theorists of much avail. Most presuppose, as interactive with rhythmic structures, concomitant pitch structures organized hierarchically in a Schenkerian or post-Schenkerian manner. Such is the case, for example, with the studies of Komar[4] and of Lehrdahl/Jackendoff[5]. The terminology of Yeston[6] is of greater formal scope, but the extent to which his formalism could carry statements of musical interest outside a tonal prolongational context is not clear.[7]

It does seem clear, in any case, that an attempt to explicate the inference of (5.2) from (5.1) in such terms would be uncomfortably problematical. Specifically, Yeston asserts axiomatically that "when considered abstractly, a faster level of motion is observed to be grouped (or meter-defined) by a slower motion from event to event on another stratum."[8] In similar vein, "any single level of motion remains uninterpreted so long as it is isolated from and unrelated to any other level of motion. . . ."[9] According to this premise, an explication of (5.2) would have

3. The notion that our perceptions of tone and time are culturally, historically and psychologically conditioned, without other "natural" basis, was forcefully championed by François Joseph Fétis (*Traité complet de la théorie et de la pratique de l'harmonie*, 3rd ed. [Paris: Braudus, 1849]; idem, *Histoire générale de la musique*, 5 vols. [Paris: Firmin-Didot, 1869–76]). (The reader who has trouble finding the third edition of the *Traité* can consult with profit the preface to the third edition, which is reprinted in all later editions.)

4. Arthur J. Komar, *Theory of Suspensions: A Study of Metrical and Pitch Relations in Tonal Music* (Princeton: Princeton University Press, 1971).

5. Fred Lehrdahl and Ray Jackendoff, "Toward a Formal Theory of Tonal Music," *Journal of Music Theory*, vol. 21, no. 1: 111–71.

6. Maury Yeston, *The Stratification of Musical Rhythm* (New Haven and London: Yale University Press, 1976).

7. See Yeston's own discussion of this issue (*Stratification*, pp. 148–53).

8. Yeston, p. 68.

9. Ibid., p. 77.

to assert that, upon hearing the stimulus of (5.1), we are somehow aware, *before* making any metric interpretation, of a "level of motion" determined by the first, third, fourth, and fifth attacks [the "half-note level" of (5.2)]; we are also aware, prior to interpretation, of a "level of motion" determined by the third and fifth attacks [the "bar lines" of (5.2)]; and only *then* do we make the metric interpretation under discussion. One notes that the actual sequence of attacks in the stimulus is not viewed here as one "level of motion"; it comprises both "quarters" and "halves" of (5.2). All of this seems strained, and I imagine that Yeston would be among the first to protest the attempt to apply his assumptions to the situation. Rather than positing preexisting levels of rhythmic activity, whose interrelations lead to a metric interpretation of (5.1), it seems more suggestive to attach theoretical priority here to a process of metric interpretation operating on (5.1) as a *Gestalt;* the "levels" of (5.2) would then be by-products of the interpreting process itself.

That is the point of view I shall explore and develop in this chapter. My approach will not preclude attributing decisive importance to dimensions other than rhythmic, tonal in particular, where that is appropriate. But it will not presuppose sonorous givens other than rhythm and, later, "accent," the latter being defined at first only formally. In this sense, the theory is classical, or rather neoclassical.

Since the theory requires a large amount of mathematical modeling, I shall develop it through a series of increasingly complex versions, hoping that the reader will be able better to follow the ideas from simpler to more elaborate models.

Version 1 of the Theory: Explication of (5.2)

We start with the series of durations (2, 3, 4, 5) which generated (5.1) and produced the response of (5.2). Let us construct a set of time points corresponding to the moments articulated by those successive durations. It will be convenient (although not necessary) to imagine the first of these points at time $t = 0$. The second articulation will then come two units later, at time $t = 2$; the third will come three units thereafter, at time $t = 5$; etc. Continuing in this manner, one constructs a set of time points (0, 2, 5, 9, 14) whose successive members span the given series of durations (2, 3, 4, 5).

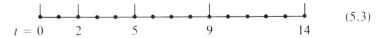

$$t = 0 \qquad 2 \qquad\quad 5 \qquad\qquad 9 \qquad\qquad\qquad 14$$

(5.3)

The figure displays the time points on a horizontal axis. Over each time point I have erected a spike of constant height; this is to model Bamberger's situation, in which an acoustic pulse of constant amplitude was produced at each point.

Listening to the stimulus, we will perceive various durational relations involving these points. Such relations will include those of the original durational series, but will not be limited to them. For instance, at time $t = 9$ we become aware not only of the duration $d = 4$, from $t = 5$ to $t = 9$, but also of the durations $d = 7$, from $t = 2$ to $t = 9$, and $d = 9$, from $t = 0$ to $t = 9$. I shall also presume here that at time $t = 9$ we still remember, in some functional sense, other durations we noted earlier, e.g., the duration $d = 3$ between $t = 2$ and $t = 5$. Let us now explore our response to the stimulus, as that response develops over four chronological stages, namely at times $t = 2, 5, 9,$ and 14.

Stage 1: $t = 2$. As yet we have experienced only one duration, $d = 2$. The notion can be modeled by (5.4a), which also indicates that we have not yet experienced any other durations, in particular any of 3, 4, 5, 7, 9, 12, or 14 units.

$d =$	2	3	4	5	7	9	12	14	(5.4a)
number of d experienced at $t = 2$	1	0	0	0	0	0	0	0	

Stage 2: $t = 5$. We now experience a duration of 3, from $t = 2$ to $t = 5$, and a duration of 5, from $t = 0$ to $t = 5$. We can update the table of Stage 1 accordingly, continuing to ''remember'' the content of that earlier table.

$d =$	2	3	4	5	7	9	12	14	(5.4b)
number of d experienced at $t = 5$	1	1	0	1	0	0	0	0	

Stage 3: $t = 9$. We now update the table of Stage 2, to accomodate our new experiences of durations 4 ($t = 5$–9), 7 ($t = 2$–9), and 9 ($t = 0$–9).

$d =$	2	3	4	5	7	9	12	14	(5.4c)
number of d experienced at $t = 9$	1	1	1	1	1	1	0	0	

Notice that at this stage we have experienced a variety of durations, but none more than once. That is, no duration predominates numerically over the others on the table. This state of affairs is about to change.

Stage 4: $t = 14$.   We update our impressions at Stage 3, with the newly experienced durations $d = 5$ ($t = 9$–14), $d = 9$ ($t = 5$–14), $d = 12$, and $d = 14$. Incrementing our count of each of these d values by 1, on the table of (5.4c), we arrive at

$d =$	2	3	4	5	7	9	12	14	(5.4d)
number of d experienced at $t = 14$	1	1	1	2	1	2	1	1	

At this stage we experience for the first time recurring durations, $d = 5$ and $d = 9$, which thereby predominate numerically over other experienced durations, giving rise to numerical "peaks" in (5.4d). My theory presumes that the numerical peaking at this particular moment of updating, $t = 14$, models our perception of an *ictus* at that moment. That is, it reflects our "hearing" the second bar line of (5.2) at that moment. I shall also presume that the specific durations whose values peak will exert a structuring influence over ones metric response at the time of such updating. More formally and generally:

ASSUMPTION 1a: *Experience of an ictus at a certain time point t is modeled by the relative peaking of one or more d values on a running d table, when that table updates at the given time.*

ASSUMPTION 1b: *The durations whose tabular values peak at that time are those involved in structuring our metric perceptions as we approach the ictus at issue.*

I shall be explicit later about the exact mathematical sense of the term "peaking"; in the given example we are studying, the idea is intuitively clear. In that example, the peaking arose as a result of the recurrence of the durations at issue in a statistical count. Later on, we shall see that a numerical value of a d argument can peak on an updating table, in an extended sense, for reasons other than statistical recurrence, while still modeling the perception of an ictus. So it seems that one should take the peaking phenomenon itself as primary in the model.

Since we did not observe the peaking phenomenon in connection with (5.4a–c), Assumption 1a involves an assertion that, in the present example, we do not experience any ictus in our listening before the last attack, at $t = 14$; hence the whole metric sense of (5.2) is completely dependent on our hearing the ictus at the last attack. This assertion seems plausible to me: I believe I hear the stimulus as much more "ametric," intuitively, when I omit the last attack (performing, that is, the time-point set 0, 2, 5, 9 only). It is hard, of course, to be sure of one's own intuition after having analyzed (5.1) so self-consciously to such an extent.

Let us now explore the pertinence of Assumption 1b to the explication of (5.2). The assumption says that when we hear the ictus at $t = 14$, our metric processing of the recent past is structured by the durations $d = 5$ and $d = 9$, the durations whose values peak on the table at that given time. The structuring role of $d = 5$ is suggested by

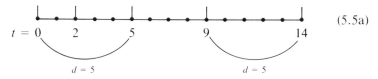

(5.5a)

Example (5.5a) displays the time points spanned by the peaking duration. I suggest that this structure sets up a metric relation, perceived at (but not until) $t = 14$, involving the four time points. It is reasonable to suppose that the relation here can be expressed as a functional proportion: Time point 0 is to time point 5 as time point 9 is to time point 14. Since time point 14 is already perceived as an ictus (according to Assumption 1a), the proportion supports hearing time point 5 as a "pseudo-ictus" by analogy, with time points 9 and 0 functioning as upbeats to the respective "downbeats" so established. In sum, the proportion suggests the metric reading of

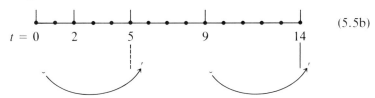

(5.5b)

The bar line at time point 5 in (5.5b) is drawn as dotted to indicate that it is both "weaker" than and qualitatively different from the bar line at time point 14. We do not hear an ictus at listening time $t = 5$, as we do at listening time $t = 14$ (the table does not peak when $t = 5$); the metric "strength" of time point 5 has been constructed in retrospect and by analogy as we listen at time $t = 14$.

From (5.5b) one can reconstruct (5.2) with a few extra observations now of a traditional sort, hitherto eschewed. The attack at time point 2 divides the time span $t = 0$–5 into roughly equal subspans: We can hear the difference as rubato here because neither of the subdurations $d = 2$ or

$d = 3$ has a metrically structural function in the sense that $d = 5$ has. Likewise the time span $t = 5-9$ involves a nonstructural duration $d = 4$ (in our present sense) that we can hear as "about equal to" $d = 5$. We will do so to iron out the measure from $t = 5$ to 14 into a "strong" half and a "weak" half. It is just here, then, that I think *Entzweiung*, acculturation, and stratification enter into the picture. But these, as I see the matter, are not responses to (5.1) as a raw stimulus. Rather they are responses to the already processed matrix of (5.5b); it is that matrix which suggests filling out and refining our metric impressions in a traditional mode. Notice again that the "ironed out" durations in this account, $d = 2, 3$, and 4, are not structurally functional for our metric interpretation in the way that $d = 5$ is.

Let us investigate the structuring role of the other duration whose value peaks at $t = 14$, namely $d = 9$. Example (5.6) is the analog of (5.5a) for this d value.

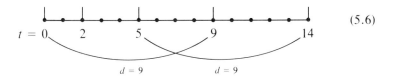

(5.6)

If we now follow the form of the argument we went through for $d = 5$, we will arrive at conclusions manifestly unsatisfactory in describing the structure asserted by (5.2). That structure does not project an upbeat–downbeat relation between time points 0 and 9, which is analogous to and derived from a similar relation between time points 5 and 14, so that the "upbeat" at 5 finds its associated downbeat (at 14) only after leapfrogging some intermediate downbeat (at 9). It would be out of place here to argue whether or not one ever could have such a sensation, in a suitable contrapuntal context. What we can observe is that there are reasonable formal grounds, within the system we are developing, for ruling out the apparent metric implications of (5.6) in favor of the implications of (5.5a), given an ictus at time point 14.

To see this, let us examine the proportional relation suggested by (5.6) without drawing any upbeat–downbeat inferences therefrom. The proportion asserts that time point 0 is to time point 9, metrically, as 5 is to 14. Now that notion is perfectly consistent with the metric situation of (5.5b). Time point 0, the first upbeat of that figure, is to 9, the second upbeat, as 5, the first downbeat, is to 14, the second downbeat. That is, $d = 9$ has a perfectly clear metric function: It spans the distance between the two "upbeats," and also between the two "downbeats" of (5.6) at the half-note level. Conceptual problems arise only when we try to read upbeat–downbeat significance into (5.6) in the same way we read such significance for (5.5a). Formally, we need only a preference rule to tell us not to make that attempt here.

The basis for such a rule is the observation that (5.5a) and (5.6) are actually only different aspects of *one* relation obtaining among the four time points 0, 5, 9, and 14. The relation can be expressed by pointing out that $5 - 0 = 14 - 9$, as in (5.5a); it can also, and equivalently, be expressed by pointing out that $9 - 0 = 14 - 5$, as in (5.6). In general, if w, x, y, and z are numerical labels for four time points in order of succession, then the numbers enjoy the relation $x - w = z - y$ if and only if they enjoy the relation $z - x = y - w$.

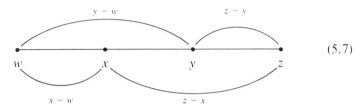

$$(5.7)$$

Supposing this to be the case, and supposing an ictus at time point z, with both the durations under discussion having peaking values there, the preference rule tells us to read the shorter duration as spanning upbeats-to-downbeats, and the longer as spanning upbeat-to-upbeat and down-beat-to-downbeat, other things being equal. From a methodological viewpoint, there is no need to support this rule by invoking similar rules stated with more familiar vocabulary. Few readers, I imagine, will have trouble supplying their own "reasons," in such terms, for the plausibility of the rule.

Let us now survey the explication of (5.2) which has just been completed. The crucial new tool we used was the "updating d table" associated with the set of time points. It is time now to be more formal about that construction. For every duration d of interest, and at every listening time t of interest, we have associated a number $W1(d, t)$, the number of occurrences of duration d up to and including time t. More formally still, $W1(d, t)$ counts the number of pairs of time points (r, s) such that $r < s \le t$, r and s are within the given time-point set, and $s - r = d$. $W1$ is thus a running temporal "interval vector" of the given time-point set, as the latter unfolds in partial stages through its own intrinsic internal chronology.[10]

---

10. The possibility of making an analogous construction for an *ordered* set of pitches or pitch classes is obvious and attractive. Notice, though, that such a set has no "intrinsic internal chronology"; its ordering involves some temporal dimension, qualitative or quantitative, extrinsic to the set itself. We could only update an unfolding of the set in that extrinsic dimension, which in itself would of course involve rhythmic considerations.

TABLE 5.1

	$d =$	2	3	4	5	7	9	12	14
value of	$t = 2$	1							
$W1(d, t)$ at	$t = 5$	1	1		1				
	$t = 9$	1	1	1	1	1	1		
	$t = 14$	1	1	1	**2**	1	**2**	1	1

$W1(d, t)$ attaches a certain "weight" to the influence of duration d at listening time t. The symbol W was chosen to convey the notion of weight. The postscript 1 of $W1$ indicates that this is the first version of a family of such weighting functions we shall explore. Table 5.1 collates (5.4a–d). The peaking values for durations $d = 5$ and $d = 9$, at listening time $t = 14$, are in boldface. We shall formalize the sense in which each of these entries of "2" on the table is a "peak," by the four following criteria:

1. The entry is greater than 1.
2. It is greater than the entry directly above it, in its column.
3. It is greater than the next nonzero entry to its left (if any), in its row.
4. It is greater than the next nonzero entry to its right (if any), in its row.

An Analytic Application

Before going on to develop extended versions of the theory, let us see what it can highlight in its present form when brought up to some music. For this purpose, I have selected the first part of Arnold Schoenberg's piano piece Op. 19, No. 6. A score of the entire piece appears as Figure 5.1.

Table 5.2 displays a partial $W1$ table for the temporal structure of the work through m. 6. I have taken $t = 0$ to label the first attack in the music, and have measured time points thereafter in notated quarters of the score. Thus $t = 13.5$, for example, occurs $13\frac{1}{2}$ quarters after the initial attack, that is, on the second eighth of m. 4. I am presuming that at least the shorter durations experienced in this music are potentially functional metrically even at the slow tempo. Table 5.2 counts, in updating fashion, all durations of up through eight quarters experienced through m. 6. I believe it is safe to exclude consideration of longer durations in this connection, at the given tempo. I emphasize in boldface those entries that meet the criteria for "peaking" enumerated at the end of the previous section. (I have not emphasized any entries in the last column, since the table does not continue to the right of that column.)

VI

FIGURE 5.1.

We can make some interesting synoptic observations from Table 5.2. Three of its columns contain three peak entries, namely the columns headed $d = 1$, $d = 3$, and $d = 7$; no other column contains more than one peak entry. That the duration of one quarter should enjoy such ongoing metric priority is not surprising in a piece for which the quarter is a notational tactus. The priorities for $d = 3$ and $d = 7$ are more surprising, and will repay later study. Note that the columns headed by $d = 2$ and $d = 4$ contain no peak entries at all, despite the notated time signature. In fact, no observed instance of $d = 2$ occurs anywhere in the music until the

TABLE 5.2

	d = 0.5	1	1.5	2	2.5	3	3.5	4	4.5	5	5.5	6	6.5	7	7.5	8
t = 3						1										
7						1		1						1		
10						2		1						2		
11		1				2		2						2		1
12.5		1	1		1	2		2			1			2		1
13.5		2	1		2	2	1	2			1		1	2		1
16		2	1		3	2	2	2		1	1	1	1	2		1
17		3	1		3	2	3	2	1	1	1	2	1	3		1
19		3	1	1	3	3	3	2	1	1	2	2	2	3		2
20		4	1	1	3	4	3	3	1	1	2	2	3	3	1	2
20.5	1	4	2	1	3	4	4	3	2	1	2	2	3	4	1	3
22	1	4	3	2	3	5	4	3	2	2	2	3	3	4	1	3

fourth-chord begins to move at $t = 19$ (the second attack of m. 5). Pre-dominant and recurrent peaking in the $d = 3$ and $d = 7$ columns does not mean that the music is "in 3" or "in 7" in any traditional sense. It means, according to Assumptions 1a and 1b, that it is recurrently thematic to experience metric weight ("ictus") three quarters, and also seven quarters, after something else. "Something else," however, was not necessarily itself an ictus. Notice that the peaks for $d = 2.5$ and $d = 3.5$, at listening times $t = 16$ and 17, are respectively a bit shorter than and a bit longer than the basic peaking duration $d = 3$.

Turning now from the columns to the rows of Table 5.2: One of those contains four peak entries modeling unique maximal functional ictus at time $t = 17$, the first attack of m. 5. Notice that this attack, which involves the fourth-chord in the left hand of the *Hauptmotiv,* occurs at a notated bar line, befitting its uniqueness. Indeed, it is one of only two attacks in the entire piece which so occur. (The other is at the beginning of m. 9, where the returning right-hand chord of the motif appears. One conjectures that the time signature may have been used to make these attacks—but not others—come out notationally "right.")

Two other rows in Table 5.2 have more than one peak entry, those headed by $t = 10$ and by $t = 20$. The former is also the first row within which any peak entries appear. The time point $t = 10$ is the second quarter of m. 3, and it is not coincidental (as we shall presently see) that the "ictus" sonority here is the same left-hand fourth-chord that was just discussed in connection with the bar line of m. 5. As for the attack at $t = 20$ (last quarter of m. 5), an assertion of metric weight here is certainly cogent in connection with the opening up of the low register and the pedal indication.

Let us now go over the various individual peaks of the table, and pertinent aspects of the music, chronologically. The peaks at $t = 10$ set up a metric interpretation for the repeated *Hauptmotiv*, via the peaking durations 3 and 7, in the fashion discussed during the last section. The asserted effect may be symbolized as in (5.8), although the bar lines are somewhat too crude here in their traditional connotations.

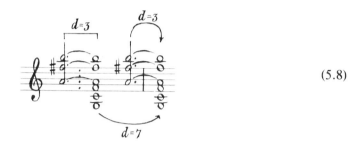

(5.8)

This matrix for the *Hauptmotiv* asserts perception, at $t = 10$ but not before, of relative weight on the left-hand chord(s); it asserts an upbeat function for the right hand chord(s), and structural emphasis on the duration of 3. The next peak on the table occurs at $t = 13.5$, the second eighth of m. 4. The peaking structural duration is 1. Just as the function of $d = 3$ was associated before with approach to the two attacks of the left-hand chord, so now the function of $d = 1$ is associated with approach to the two attacks of the octave D-sharp, as in (5.9).

(5.9)

The sense of ictus [the bar line of (5.9), again too crude a symbol] is less powerful here. (It does make good sense of the dynamic mark on the second of the lower D-sharps.) Notice that I have drawn no dotted bar line on (5.9) before the first D-sharp attack. This is because there is no peak on the table for $d = 2.5$ (the distance between D-sharp attacks) at $t = 13.5$, so the sort of metric proportion in the preceding section and operative in (5.8) is not fully functional here. $W1(2.5, 13.5) = 2$ is not a peak specifically because it fails to surpass $W1(3, 13.5) = 2$. The structuring force of $d = 2.5$ cannot (yet) overcome the already established force of $d = 3$: In more traditional terms, we are reluctant to put a "dotted bar line" involving $d = 2.5$ before the third quarter of m. 3, at the expense of the already established "solid bar line" involving $d = 3$ that we placed before the second quarter of m. 3.

This situation changes as the second phrase begins. The attack of the right-hand chord at $t = 16$, coming 2.5 quarters after the last D-sharp attack, now does create a temporary peak for $d = 2.5$ at the expense of $d = 3$. It thereby threatens to undermine not only the thematic rhythmic matrix of (5.8), but also an important concomitant sense of the *Hauptmotiv*, which had established right-to-left hands in an upbeat-to-downbeat relation. Now $d = 2.5$, with weight on the right-hand chord (and D-sharp), threatens to take over the music at the expense of $d = 3$, with weight on the left-hand chord.

Just on the heels of this dramatically tense moment comes the big pulse at $t = 17$, the bar line of m. 5, which I discussed earlier. The left-hand chord reasserts its metric priority over the right hand with a vengeance. This assertion, however, does not involve the duration 3 that the right hand has just threatened, at least not directly. That is, the value for $d = 3$ does not peak at $t = 17$; instead there are peaks for $d = 1, d = 3.5, d = 6$, and $d = 7$. Let us examine each.

The new peak for $d = 1$ at this moment is created by the rhythmic transformation of the *Hauptmotiv*: Right-hand-to-left-hand is now one quarter instead of three. Thus, while it abandons $d = 3$, the ictus on the left-hand chord forcefully expropriates $d = 1$, in exchange, from the D-sharp to which $d = 1$ had earlier "belonged" [in (5.9)].

The peak for $d = 3.5$, it was earlier suggested, can be regarded as balancing the $d = 2.5$ peak about $d = 3$; the latter duration will peak again later on. But $d = 3.5$ also has an interesting and suggestive function here in its own right, along with $d = 7$. Example (5.10) displays the structure.

(5.10)

The dotted and solid bar lines on the figure are those from (5.8) and (5.9), plus a new double bar representing the big ictus at $t = 17$. The three bar lines that are not dotted span two "measures" of 3.5 quarters each; this involves all the analyzed strong ictus in the piece so far. The dotted bar line, it will be recalled, was "reconstructed" at $t = 10$, seven quarters after; now that the left-hand chord has recurred yet again, here with even greater metric weight, it is again exactly seven quarters later. So powerful is this structuring that it leads one to conjecture understanding the rhythm of the opening *Hauptmotiv* presentations as a rubato for a steady rhythm in regular "beats" of 3.5 units. It seems safe to say, at least, that the opening of the piece should be understood as including the possibility for such a reading. Of course such regularity, which would well-nigh force the piece into a regular meter in a very traditional sense, following (5.10), does not in fact emerge in the music: Even by the end of m. 6, $d = 3$ does reassert its power. Still, the potential for such a reading, at listening time $t = 17$, is striking. The fact that the music rejects that reading in the sequel is arguably related to the vanishing of the left-hand chord and the *Hauptmotiv* itself after $t = 17$.

The less powerful peaking of the value for $d = 6$ at $t = 17$ is tied up in a proportional relation with the peaking of the value for $d = 1$ there [see (5.11)]. An extended form of our preference rule analyses the former peaking as subordinate in function to the latter.

$$(5.11)$$

The low E–D at $t = 20$ carried peaks for $d = 1$ and $d = 3$. I hear the new instance of $d = 1$, inflecting $t = 20$ from the quarter before, as a rhythmic echo of the earlier approach to the ictus at $t = 17$ from a quarter before: The secondary ictus at $t = 20$ "prolongs" in this respect the rhythmic character of the stronger earlier ictus, just as the expanding chain of fourths up to $t = 20$ "prolongs" the intervallic character of that event.

The peaking of $d = 3$ at $t = 20$, however, has quite a different function. Specifically, it restores the primacy of $d = 3$, which had been so forcefully contested by the 3.5 associations with the $t = 17$ ictus [as in (5.10)]. And it restores that primacy in conjunction with an attack on the lowest sonority so far in the music, a conjunction which was also characteristic of the earlier peaking for $d = 3$, at $t = 10$, and which had been lost when the left-hand fourth-chord changed its allegiance at $t = 17$, from $d = 3$ to $d = 3.5$. The new instance of $d = 3$ that creates the peak at $t = 20$ is, in fact, exactly the span from $t = 17$ to $t = 20$.[11] This reassertion of $d = 3$ is echoed as the phrase cadences by yet one more peaking of that duration's count, at $t = 22$ (the F-sharp attack).

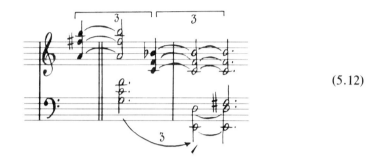

(5.12)

Meanwhile, the G-sharp at $t = 20.5$ has kept the implications of (5.10) also reechoing, via the temporary repeaking of $t = 7$ and the new addition to the count of $d = 3.5$ in syncopated contention with $d = 3$

(5.13)

This finishes our survey of all the peak values on Table 5.2. I shall eschew the temptation to draw speculative general inferences about "atonal meter," and content myself with the observation that the present mode of discourse, even using so simple a version of the theory, has enabled us to formulate and discuss some interesting and not immediately obvious ideas about the rhythmic structure of the passage under examination. The fermata in m. 6 and the new activity in m. 7–8 would complicate unduly a continuation of the analysis in such detail through the rest of the piece. One might still note that the last attack in m. 8 comes four quarters after the first attack in m. 7, and also three quarters before the bar line chord of

11. The attribution of such importance to $d = 3$ here, at the expense of $d = 1$, apparently violates the preference rule. The rule, however, contained a provision for "other things being equal." By this point in the music, as the present discussion has just emphasized, $d = 3$ is not a neutral, but a highly charged thematic element of the piece.

m. 9. The latter, the right-hand chord of the *Hauptmotiv*, thus increments the counts of both $d = 3$ and $d = 7 (= 4 + 3)$ upon its arrival; in this respect its metric function is now analogous to that originally manifested by the LH chord of m. 3 (at $t = 10$).

Version 2 of the Theory: Nonrhythmic "Accent"

The reader may have noticed that the weighing function $W1$, conceived as as a running temporal interval vector for an unfolding set of time points, does not at all utilize the notion I introduced in connection with (5.3), imagining a spike over each point of that set to symbolize an equal accent at each time point. A mathematical model for that notion is provided by the function $f1(t)$; this function assigns the value 0 to any time point t that is not in the desired set, and assigns the value 1 to each time point t that is in the set. We can express $W1$ formally in terms of the function $f1$, and for purposes of extending our theory, it will be useful to do so. The pertinent equation is

$$W1(d, t) = \sum_{s \leq t} f1(s)f1(s - d) \tag{5.14}$$

In this formula the capital sigma, qualified by $s \leq t$, means "the sum over all values of s that are less than or equal to (the given time point) t." What we are to sum, over those values of s, are the individual products $f1(s)f1(s - d)$. For each such s, the corresponding individual product will vanish if s is not in the time-point set, since $f1(s)$ will then equal 0. The product will also vanish if $s - d$ is not in the time-point set, since $f1(s - d)$ will then equal 0. So the product $f1(s)f1(s - d)$ will not contribute to the overall sum in (5.14) unless both s and $s - d$ are in the given time-point set. In that case, $f1(s)$ and $f1(s - d)$ will each be 1, and their product will be 1. A summand of 1 is thus contributed to the overall sum for each instance of s and $s - d$ both in the time-point set, with $s \leq t$. The overall sum, that is, tabulates the number of pairs (r, s) such that $r = s - d$, r and s are both in the set, and $s \leq t$. This number is precisely $W1(d, t)$ as defined earlier.

We shall call the function $f1$ a "scanning function" for the stimulus under discussion. We can imagine $f1$ as scanning through the time variable s, reading (or emitting) a blip of unit intensity every time it encounters an s in the time-point set.

Such a notion can easily be extended to accommodate the idea of accenting certain time points from the set over others. We simply replace $f1$ by a more sophisticated scanning function $f2$. This $f2$ assigns zero value to time points not in the set; if s is in the set, then $f2$ reads (or emits) at time s a blip of relative intensity $f2(s)$.

For example, let us imagine producing the same stimulus as that of (5.1), only with pronounced dynamic accents on the second and fourth attacks. We will of course have the metric sensation of (5.15), overriding the sense of (5.2).

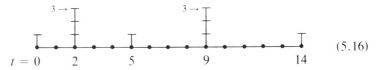

(5.15)

To explicate the phenomenon consistently, we construct the accented scanning function $f2$. We shall suppose that $f2$ reads or emits a blip of unit intensity at the unaccented time points 0, 5, and 14. At $t = 2$ and $t = 9$ (on the second and fourth attacks) we shall let $f2$ read or emit a blip of triple that intensity: $f2(2) = f2(9) = 3$.[12] We can graph $f2$ as in (5.16).

$$
\begin{array}{ccccc}
3 \rightarrow & & & 3 \rightarrow & \\
\end{array}
$$

$t = 0 \qquad 2 \qquad 5 \qquad 9 \qquad 14$

(5.16)

The structure of (5.16) already explicates the sense of (5.15) perfectly well in traditional fashion. Nevertheless it will be worth exploring how our present theory analyzes the situation. From the scanning function $f2$ we construct a new weighting function $W2$ by extending the formula of (5.14) to that of

$$W2(d, t) = \sum_{s \leq t} f2(s)f2(s - d)$$

(5.17)

Weight function $W2$, like $W1$, counts up the number of occurrences of duration d within the time-point set as of listening time t. But now, for each instance of $s \leq t$ with s and $s - d$ in the set, the importance of that instance is itself weighted proportional to the amount of accent at time s and the amount of accent at time $s - d$. Instead of simply contributing an increment of 1 to the overall sum, the product $f2(s)f2(s - d)$ contributes a greater or lesser amount, proportional to the accentual significance of s and $s - d$. In this way, it is possible for durations that occur less often to have greater $W2$ values than others, provided that the time points spanning such durations are sufficiently accented. Table 5.3, for example, displays a $W2$ table for the scanning function $f2$ of (5.16).

Table 5.3 is unable to display "peaking" behavior at $t = 2$, since it only

12. This is a modest psychoacoustic gain.

TABLE 5.3

$d =$	2	3	4	5	7	9	12	14
$t =$ 2	3							
5	3	3		1				
9	3	3	3	1	**9**	3		
14	3	3	3	4	9	4	3	1

starts tabulating there. (Later versions of the theory, allowing us to analyze our responses for continuous values of t, in particular for those t between 0 and 2, could remedy this defect.) So we cannot yet explicate the perceived ictus at $t = 2$. But the table does reflect very well the perceived ictus at $t = 9$, by the abrupt and pronounced peaking of $W2(7, 9)$. The peak explicates well not only the ictus but also the structuring function of $d = 7$ in approaching it, that duration spanning the "measure" of (5.15) between time points 2 and 9. Note that $d = 7$ occurs only once between points of the time set; its weight on Table 5.3 at $t = 9$ arises not from its frequency of recurrence, but rather from the accent attached to the time points that span it. The formulation of Assumptions 1a and 1b, however, remains the same as far as the new mathematical model is concerned: Perceived ictus at time $t = 9$ is reflected by a peaking $W2$ value at that time, and that d whose value peaks there ($d = 7$) is crucially involved in the metric structuring of our sensations approaching the ictus.

Notice, at time $t = 14$ on Table 5.3, how the other values in the row are beginning to "smooth out" the peak of $W2(7, 9) = W2(7, 14) = 9$. That is, the weight of 9 in the fourth row of the figure is a less pronounced maximum for that row than it was for the third row. This reflects the structuring influence of (5.2), trying to assert itself at $t = 14$ in opposition to the accentual implications of (5.15).

The last observation suggests that by altering the amounts of accent within the scanning function $f2$ we should be able to predict and analyze stimuli that are varyingly ambivalent as regards the metric readings of (5.2) and (5.15). For instance, bringing the value of $f2(2)$ down to 1.5, and the value of $f2(9)$ down to 2, as in (5.18), will produce the $W2$ table of Table 5.4; the latter still has a peak at $W2(7, 9)$, but a peak of much less prominence than that of Table 5.3.

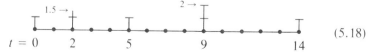

$$t = 0 \qquad 2 \qquad\qquad 5 \qquad\qquad 9 \qquad\qquad 14 \tag{5.18}$$

Furthermore, the fourth row of Table 5.4 completely "wipes out" the metric prominence of $d = 7$, allowing $d = 5$ and $d = 9$ equal weight at lis-

TABLE 5.4

$d =$	2	3	4	5	7	9	12	14
$t =$ 2	1.5							
5	1.5	1.5		1				
9	1.5	1.5	2	1	3	2		
14	1.5	1.5	2	3	3	3	1.5	1

tening time $t = 14$. This predicts that, in hearing a stimulus corresponding to (5.18), a slight preference for the interpretation of (5.15) at listening time $t = 9$ (on the fourth attack) will be followed by a state of complete ambivalence as regards the interpretations of (5.2) and (5.15), when the fifth attack is heard at time $t = 14$. One is tempted to ask qualified psychologists to run experimental games on this basis, testing the predictions of the theory. At this stage, however, the theory may still be too crude to be used for such numerical fine tuning beyond very straightforward situations.

As yet we have used the scanning function $f2$ to model only dynamic accents. In this connection, it has been supposed that the numerical values of the function should be assigned to correspond to the relative physical amplitudes of the "blips" in question. Then the logarithms of those numbers would correspond, roughly, to relative levels of perceived loudness. But the supposition may be wrong or at least too crude. We are free mathematically, of course, to assign $f2$ values, in relation to a given stimulus, as perception theory may suggest.

One could also consider using the numerical values of $f2$ to model levels of "accent" in various musical dimensions other than dynamic. For instance, the example of (5.19), performed without undue fluctuation in the nonnotated musical dimensions, produces the metric impression of (5.15) clearly enough, projecting the effect of the "accents" (in some sense) at time points 2 and 9. In that sense, something like the scanning function $f2$ of (5.16) is intuitively relevant to our perception of "accent" in the frequency domain. But just what numbers should we assign to $f2$ at the specific times $t = 0, 2, 5, 9,$ and 14, to reflect our perceptions of the relative pitch accents at those moments? Putting the question another way: Just what do we mean by "accent" in connection with the attack points of (5.19), and how is it to be measured numerically?

(5.19)

Version 3 of the Theory:
The Scanning Function as a Model of Perception;
Continuous Scanning; A Rising-Entropy Model

Until now, we have had no problems treating the scanning function as a model for an acoustical stimulus. The questions arising in connection with (5.19), however, make it impossible for us to maintain that attitude. We must instead imagine the function to be modeling some aspect of our perceptual processing of the stimulus.

So far, also, the stimuli under investigation have been finite families of discrete events. In distinction now, the stimulus of (5.19) (as a pressure-wave or voltage signal) is active not simply at time points 0, 2, 5, 9, and 14, but rather over the continuous time span extending from sometime before $t = 0$ to sometime after $t = 14$. Even though the signal is relatively unchanging while sustaining its steady states between attack points, perceptual processing is active and developing during those times. As a general rule, it is possible for processing to be active even at times when a stimulus is momentarily completely silent. In sum, we must conceive the scanning function, for the phenomenon under study here, as taking on values over a continuous span of time, while it models some aspect of our perceptual processing.

A good point of departure for the study of that processing is supplied by the technique of "time–frequency analysis." Most readers have probably seen spectrograms constructed by that method: They are used, for instance, to picture "visible speech." A time axis runs horizontally from left to right, and a frequency axis rises vertically over it on the page. Within this coordinate grid, various regions are shaded lighter or darker. The darkness of the shading at time t and frequency x is, loosely speaking, proportional to the relative amount of energy $E(x, t)$ with which frequency x appears in the signal at time t.[13]

The locution is loose first because a frequency, involving quasi-repetitive behavior of an aspect of a signal, needs a certain amount of time in which to "speak"; it can be perceived as present over that span, but not at one instant, or indeed even over too short a span. The locution is also inexact for perceptual modeling because of certain limitations in the auditory process itself, as it filters an acoustical stimulus. Under these conditions, one can interpret the relation of an energy spectogram to perception

13. A good exposition of the pertinent techniques, directed at musicians, can be found in a short study by Werner Meyer-Eppler (*The Mathematic–Acoustical Fundamentals of Electrical Sound Composition*, trans. H.A.G. Nathan, technical trans. TT-608 [Ottawa: National Research Council of Canada, 1956]). My "energy" spectrogram is the square of his "amplitude" spectrogram.

as follows: Suppose that the signal starts at time zero, and suppose you have been listening from that time up until time t; then $E(x, t)$ is the relative density with which you will perceive frequencies near x as having been present in the sound shortly before time t, taking into account your listening from time zero on.[14]

If we make a vertical cross-cut of the spectrogram at listening time t, the way in which the values of $E(x, t)$ are distributed over the various x at that time will reflect the extent of organization or disorganization of our listening experience then, as regards the frequency domain. To the extent the E values peak and gather about a certain frequency x, to that extent our frequency perception is more "organized" at time t. In contrast, greater "disorganization" is modeled by a more uniform distribution of E values over a wider continuous band, or wider bands, of frequencies.[15]

A numerical value can be computed to measure the precise amount of "disorganization" or "uncertainty" in our frequency-perception at listening time t, compared with other listening times. The quantity is conventionally denoted by the letter H. Since H varies here according to the listening time t, we shall consider perceptual disorganization in the frequency domain, in this situation, to be a varying function $H(t)$ of that time. The mathematical formalities are developed in a footnote.[16]

If we graph the values of H, t varying from before the onset to after the conclusion of (5.19), we obtain a curve with the general features of Figure 5.2, which is highly simplified.

14. For the mathematically minded: If $p(t)$ is the acoustic pressure signal as a function of time, the function $C(x, t)$ will be here defined as the integral, s varying from a pertinent starting point (or minus infinity) to time t, of the integrand $p(s) \exp[-(t - s)h] \cos[2\pi(t - s)] \, ds$. The constant h in the integrand (about equal to 40) represents a filtering property of the ear. It is the reciprocal of Meyer–Eppler's "analysis interval" (*Fundamentals*, pp. 9–10). The function $S(x, t)$ will be defined here as an analogous integral, using sin instead of cos in the integrand. The function $E(x, t)$ we are considering is the sum of the squares of $C(x, t)$ and $S(x, t)$.

15. We shall not go deeply here into certain sophisticated problems that arise when a fundamental frequency is accompanied by higher partial frequencies that fuse with it into one unified sensation of "tone." We can avoid the problems here by stipulating that timbre is to be considered relatively simple and invariant over the passage at issue. We must also, as already suggested, assume that the attacks of these notes are not highly accented dynamically. Such accents would not only make it hard to ignore dynamic variation when studying the metric implications of the passage, they would also introduce transient high frequencies into the signal, which would confuse and complicate the time–frequency analysis itself. To avoid such problems, one might think of the passage as being played by a tenor recorder at a moderate dynamic level.

16. Let $A(t)$ be the integral, with respect to x, of the function $E(x, t)$ at time t. The function $P(x, t) = E(x, t)/A(t)$ is then a probability density function for the variable x, at the given time t. The amount of disorganization associated with P at time t, $H(t)$, is the integral with respect to x of the integrand $-P(x, t) \log P(x, t)$.

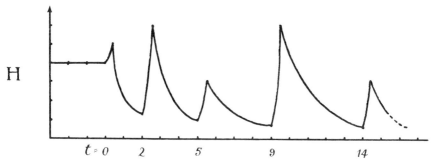

H

$t = 0$ 2   5   9   14

FIGURE 5.2.

A relatively high level of frequency-disorganization is presumed before $t = 0$, owing to the rather homogeneous distribution of energy among various (low-intensity) frequencies in the environment and the body of the listener, present in the "silence" before the first attack. The low intensity of the sound is not relevant to its organization or disorganization, as regards the frequency domain itself.

The initial disruption of this ongoing state of affairs by a new, as yet unanalyzed stimulus is responsible for a slight (but only slight) rise in uncertainty just after $t = 0$. (Once more, we should note the assumption of a smooth inception for the first tone, minimizing the effect of dynamic accent and transient high frequencies at this moment.) The phenomenon persists briefly, up to a time which we will call $t = 0^+$. Immediately after that, the level of disorganization plummets downwards, as our perception begins to gather and organize energy in the stimulus close to frequency G4. This process continues up to $t = 2$. While H continues to decline over that time span, its rate of decline becomes progressively more and more gradual. This models the fact that our growing "certainty" as to frequency G4 more and more confirms an already strong impression of "sureness," rather than organizing a hitherto disorganized perception.

At $t = 2$, the level of disorganization shoots up again as F-sharp begins to sound. The stimulus we have been processing so far stops, and a new one, as yet unanalyzed, begins. Beyond that, when our perception begins to process the new sensation, we discover that it is incompatible with the hitherto perceived gathering of energy about G4, a sense of frequency organization that carries on a bit past $t = 2$ with some inertia. Such incompatibility raises the level of uncertainty even more, up until a time $t = 2^+$, when the perceptual apparatus begins to reorganize frequency energies about a peak at F-sharp.[17] From $t = 2^+$ to $t = 5$, the value of H declines

17. Observe the "smears" on Meyer–Eppler's Figure 5 (*Fundamentals*, p. 31). They arise from just such a change in sounding tone.

again in the manner discussed before, in connection with the time span $t = 0^+$ to 2.

At $t = 5$, when the second F-sharp sounds, uncertainty begins to rise again. As with the situation at $t = 2$, an old stimulus stops and a new one, as yet unanalyzed, begins. But, in distinction to the earlier situation, incipient analysis of the new sensation reveals that we will *not* have to revise our residual impressions of energy gathering about the "old" frequency peak. As a result, although the level of disorganization rises from $t = 5$ to 5^+, it does not rise so high at 5^+ as it did at 2^+, and it will not rise so fast, from 5 to 5^+, as it did from 2 to 2^+.

Discussion of the rest of the H curve would proceed in a similar vein. The situation from $t = 9$ to 9^+ is analogous to that from $t = 2$ to 2^+; the span from 14 to 14^+ is analogous to that from 5 to 5^+. It should be stressed here that the recent discussion of Figure 5.2 is not simply a flight of metaphorical fancy: It reflects quite formal numerical aspects of a computed mathematical structure. Of course my decision to employ the spectrogram, my decision to derive the H function therefrom, and the way I interpret the resulting picture are all in some sense "metaphorical," as is any mathematical or scientific model. Still, the time-frequency technique leading to the spectrogram has a wide acceptance among psychoacousticians, and the mathematical formula for measuring "disorganization" invoked here is well established.

The H curve of Figure 5.2, with its bumps shortly after the time points of the original set, seems related to the scanning function we wish to construct for metric analysis. But it will not do to use the function $H(t)$ itself for that purpose. First of all, the numerical values for H are mathematically determined only up to within addition or subtraction of an arbitrary constant quantity. In effect, we are free to select a mathematically arbitrary "normal level" of disorganization here, to which we assign H value zero. Other H values will then be positive or negative according whether the situations from which they arise are, respectively, more or less disorganized than the "normal" situation.

The psychoacoustical implications of Figure 5.2 suggest that a logical choice for such a "normal" level of disorganization here is the value of H preceding $t = 0$ on the figure, that is, the average level of frequency disorganization associated with background noise in the ear. But this would make the high values of the graph close to zero (positive or negative), whereas the low values would be quite large in a negative sense, and would be present during much of the time span involved. If s and $s - d$ are times when the putative scanning function $f3 = H$ is high, then, the product $f3(s)f3(s - d)$ would be close to zero, not contributing much to the value of $W3$. And if $H = f3$ is low at times s and $s - d$ (which is the case for a preponderance of s and d arguments), the product of the two substantially negative numbers $f3(s)$ and $f3(s - d)$ would be a substantially large positive number, contributing greatly to a positive value for $W3$. (I am supposing for now that we know how to construct a continuous weighting function $W3$ from a continuous scanning function $f3$, and that the considerations under discussion are pertinent.) In this manner, the effect of the bumps on Figure 5.2 would be to create "troughs" rather than "peaks" in the structure of $W3$.

To approach a more satisfactory candidate for $f3$, we shall first consider H', the derivative of H. This is the function $H'(t)$ that measures the rate at which H is changing at time t. The derivative H' is more or less positive when H is growing respectively faster or slower; it is more or less negative when H is declining faster or slower; and it is zero when H is changing from growth to decay (peaking), or when H is changing from decay to growth (troughing), or when H is not changing at all. One can observe these features in comparing the graph of H' (Figure 5.3) with that of H (Figure 5.2). It may also be useful to go over the discussion of Figure 5.2 again, now while inspecting the pertinent features of the H' curve.

The rate at which H changes is independent of the arbitrary "normal level" of disorganization recently discussed; referring to H' rather than to H solves the methodological problems arising from that aspect of H. For example, the H' value preceding $t = 0$ is zero, reflecting the fact that H is (essentially) unchanging during that time span, whatever numerical value we give it. We shall see later how the idea of associating the rate-of-

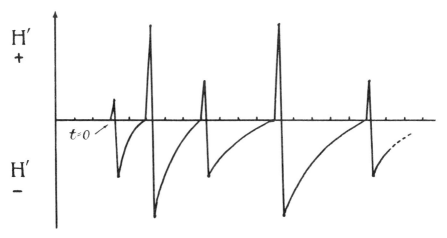

FIGURE 5.3.

change-in-uncertainty with a scanning function is also suggestive in other contexts.

However, H' itself here is still not a completely suitable candidate for a scanning function $f3$. If we try to use it as such, we shall encounter a problem already confronted before: Function $f3$ will have substantially negative values at many times and, if s and $s - d$ are two such times, the product $f3(s)f3(s - d)$ can make a substantially positive contribution to a $W3$ value we do not want large.

We can solve the formal modeling problem simply by chopping off the negative portion of Figure 5.3. We shall then hypothesize, as our desired scanning function, the function $f3(t)$ which is zero whenever $H'(t)$ is negative or zero, and which equals $H'(t)$ whenever the latter quantity is positive. This function has the sort of structure graphed in Figure 5.4, which simply cuts the bottom off Figure 5.3.

This function clearly produces very well a continuous version of the sort of "accent" structure projected by (5.16) and (5.18) earlier. Because the function has the intuitively desired shape, while still measuring exact numerical quantities, it is reasonable to entertain an assumption that it is measuring something that underlies our metric sensations. This is also not implausible psychologically, assuming that H and H' are pertinent in some way to our perceptual processing. The implication, when we ignore the negative values of H', is that our sense of metric structuring here is based only on those time spans during which we are actively receiving and trying to organize a new sensation in the pertinent domain; we do not mark those time spans during which we are coasting along, essentially only further confirming an already well-established organizational steady-state.

The term "entropy" is in current vogue as a synonym for what we have discussed as "disorganization" or "uncertainty" in the recent text. The

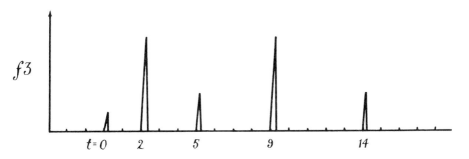

FIGURE 5.4.

function $f3$ of Figure 5.4 thus measures the rate of change of entropy wherever entropy is on the rise (H' positive). Where entropy is steady or zero (H' zero or negative), $f3$ reads or emits a zero value. I shall refer to the function as a "rising-entropy model" for scanning the stimulus of (5.19).

To obtain a weighting function $W3$ from $f3$, we can proceed by analogy with our earlier constructions. We shall specifically take $W3(d, t)$ to be the integral, over all values of $s \leq t$, of the integrand $f3(s)f3(s - d)$. For those unfamiliar with calculus, suffice it to say that the "integral" here is a standard analogy for a sum, in cases where one has to deal with a continuum, rather than a discrete family, of summands.

The integral $W3(d, t)$ takes on values over a continuous two-dimensional domain of durations d and listening times t. To visualize a three-dimensional graph of $W3$, one can imagine a continuous d axis running from left to right at the top of a page, and a continuous t axis running from top to bottom. The varying values of $W3$ can then be visualized as forming a relief map erected over the plane of the page, coming out from the page toward the reader. Each number of the $W2$ table of Table 5.3 earlier (q.v.) could represent the relative height of a hill or mountain on the $W3$ map, whose summit is at the indicated d and t location. The values of $W3$ will trough elsewhere, among these lesser and greater peaks. The lesser peaks can be interpreted as "foothills" whose summits accent all durations and times involving any pairs of attacks of the stimulus, as opposed to all other durations and times. The greater peaks are "mountains" corresponding to the larger "peaking" entries on the earlier $W1$ and $W2$ tables; we attach more importance to these mountains in making a metric interpretation than we do to the foothills. Similar criteria to those invoked before for "peaking" could be invoked to determine formally what summits here were "mountains" and what ones were "foothills," as they relate among themselves in a given neighborhood of the map.

More on Rising-Entropy Models; Rhythmic Accent

A rising-entropy model for frequency perception could be used to provide a continuous scanning function for the stimulus of the first two sections, approximating the form of (5.3) by some $f3$ of the sort just constructed. Each acoustic pulse, in the stimulus under consideration, could be analyzed as an abrupt burst of energy over a wide band of frequencies, and the spectrogram-cum-entropy methods of the preceding section would carry through to produce an $f3$ of the desired form. Such a continuous approximation to (5.3) is useful in explicating how we would perceive substantially the same effect, even if the exact time points of the stimulus were slightly displaced by a syncopating rubato.

A similar approach would not work, however, for an attempt to use a frequency–disorganization model to approximate the form of (5.16), given the dynamic accents of the associated stimulus there. That model is sensitive only to the relative amplitudes of frequencies at each given listening time; it does not compare such amplitudes at different times, to distinguish dynamic accents. So the $f3/W3$ model of the preceding section should not be considered to generalize the $f2/W2$ model of the fourth section; rather, both those models generalize the $f1/W1$ model, each in a different way. It is conceivable that a more sophisticated use of spectrogram structure might be able to construct a model that generalized both $f2/W2$ and $f3/W3$. However, I do not intuit a method for approaching such a construction at present. In any case, a broader model would not necessarily be more useful for the analysis of a particular stimulus or musical passage. For instance, it would be very cumbersome to invoke such a super-spectrogram model in connection with the remarks made earlier on the Schoenberg piece, or for discussing metric implications adhering to the dynamic accents studied on pages 118–120.

While it is not completely general, the model of Part V does nevertheless suggest investigating rising-entropy models for other situations, involving varying levels of organization and disorganization in other acoustical and musical domains. The notion seems of interest, for example, in connection with the analysis of purely rhythmic accents.

Let us consider, for instance, a stimulus emitting pulses of uniform intensity, in a brisk tempo, at time points 0, 1, 2, 3, 5, 6, 7, 9, 10, etc. The method of pages 104–110 is not adequate here for explicating the presence of "rhythmic accents" at time points 3 and 7. To explore this a bit, we can construct an $f1$, as in (5.20), and the associated $W1$ table of Table 5.5.

$$t = 0 \quad 1 \quad 2 \quad 3 \quad \quad 5 \quad 6 \quad 7 \quad \quad 9 \quad 10 \qquad \text{etc.} \qquad (5.20)$$

Table 5.5 is seriously defective in modeling our metric response to the stimulus. It fails to model clearly the perceived ictus at time points 3 and 7. It does provide peak entries at those times, but it also provides analogous peaks at time points 2, 6, and 10. The table fails to peak at $t = 7$ and $d = 4$; we should certainly expect such a peak there, since the rhythmic accents at time points 3 and 7 appear four time units apart.

One is tempted to use an $f2/W2$ model, to reflect our perception of "rhythmic accents" here. Clearly the scanning function we want should look less like (5.20) and more like (5.21).

TABLE 5.5

$d =$	1	2	3	4	5	6	7	8	9	10	etc.
$t = $ 1	1										
2	2	1									
3	3	2	1								
5	3	3	2	1	1						
6	4	3	3	2	2	1					
7	5	4	3	3	3	2	1				
9	5	5	4	4	3	3	2	1	1		
10	6	5	5	5	4	3	3	2	2	1	
etc.											

$$\text{etc.} \qquad (5.21)$$

But by what right have we extended the vertical lines over $t = 3$ and $t = 7$ on that figure? What criterion, other than intuitive whimsy, are we using to assign, or even to conceive assigning, exact and varying numerical lengths to the various vertical lines of the figure? Sensible answers to these questions were immediately forthcoming in our earlier study of dynamic accent. Here, as in the case of frequency changes, the problems must be confronted explicitly. And, as in the case of frequency changes, a rising-entropy model seems attractive in developing a hypothetical solution.

To construct such a model, we shall first presume that the ongoing peaking of Table 5.5 within the $d = 1$ column from $t = 2$ onward models a sense in which we will "mark time" here using discrete minibeats one unit apart. (We can "rubato" this assumption using a continuous model, along the lines discussed earlier in the present section. We shall pick up the idea again later, as a refinement of the present model.) In particular, now, we suppose that we will "mark" time points 4 and 8, as well as 1, 2, 3, 5, etc. We can then investigate our sense of rhythmic "organization" or "disorganization" at each marked time point. Example (5.22) graphs the overall picture.

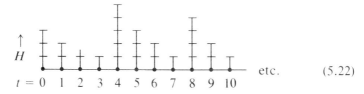

$$\text{etc.} \qquad (5.22)$$

As we listen to the successive pulses at time points 0, 1, 2, and 3, our sense of rhythmic organization increases, and H values decrease correspondingly. (There are various mathematical models that could provide exact numerical proportions for the H values here, depending on just which feature(s) of the signal one considers as "recurrent" through time point 3.) At $t = 4$, which we mark, we abruptly experience no pulse. This disruption of the established and anticipated pattern creates a sharp rise in the level of perceived disorganization. (Again, various plausible mathematical models would assign specific numbers to the exact level.) As the regular pulses resume, over time points 5 through 7, our perception of rhythmic disorder subsides from the height of $H(4)$. Then, at the marked $t = 8$, perceived disorder again becomes greater, as the reestablished pattern of regular pulses is broken once more. The value of $H(8)$ will not be so great as was $H(4)$, since the earlier disruptive event will exercise a somewhat organizing effect upon our impression of the similar later one.

In this fashion, we can graph a rising and falling entropy, for each discrete marked time point of the stimulus. To continue constructing a rising-entropy model, we have now to consider H', the rate of change of H per mark, as that quantity is associated with the marked time points. The rate of change corresponds to the differences between values of H at successive marked times. Two plausible mathematical models are available; we shall have to choose between them. For model 1 we could take $H'(t) = H(t) - H(t - 1)$ at the marked time t. This says that H "is changing" more or less, at time t, depending on how big or small $H(t)$ is when compared to the value of H at the *last* marked time. For model 2 we could take $H'(t) = H(t + 1) - H(t)$. This says that H "is changing" more or less, at time t, depending on how small or big $H(t)$ is compared to the value H will take on at the *next* marked time. Model 1 will put large positive values for H' at time points 4 and 8; model 2 will put those values at time points 3 and 7. Clearly, model 2 is our choice. The graph of H', using that model, is displayed in (5.23) below. Notice that we cannot compute $H'(10) = H(11) - H(10)$ in this model: We do not yet know what $H(11)$ will be. The spike of length "a" at time point 3 is longer than the spike of length "b" at time point 7, since (as discussed before) the lack of a pulse at $t = 4$ was more discombobulating than the lack of a pulse at $t = 8$; $H(4)$ is greater than $H(8)$, and $H'(3)$ is accordingly greater than $H'(7)$.

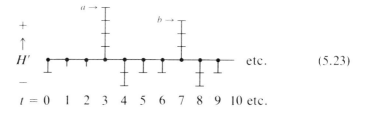

(5.23)

One may at first feel uncomfortable about the implications of Model 2. It seems to say that we perceive "at time t" a quantity $H'(t)$ that involves another quantity, $H(t + 1)$, which has not yet been perceived. Actually it is the tense-system of English verbs that is causing the discomfort: The language cannot convey very well the conceptual structure of the formal model. Each marked t on (5.23) represents not a "present" listening time, but our memory at time $t + 1$ of the recently past time t, as processed by comparison with "presently" experienced events. The propriety of such a notion can be appreciated if we ask ourselves: "Is" there a rhythmic accent at time point 10? Clearly we cannot answer this question in any way until we have listened through time point 11, whereupon the question, more properly, becomes: "Was" there (in the recent past) a rhythmic accent at time point 10? Model 2 reflects this aspect of our perception here very clearly. We must of course assume a brisk tempo: Beyond a certain limit, the durations between successive marked time points become so great that the past times in question are no longer "recent" as of the next mark.

Continuing to follow the method of the preceding section, we shall now chop away the negative spikes from (5.23) and consider the result (5.24), as a putative scanning function.

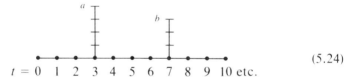

$$t = 0 \quad 1 \quad 2 \quad 3 \quad 4 \quad 5 \quad 6 \quad 7 \quad 8 \quad 9 \quad 10 \text{ etc.} \tag{5.24}$$

This is not yet satisfactory, however. Though the graphed function does accent time points 3 and 7, it takes on no other nonzero values. Consequently its associated W table would have one unique nonzero entry, $W(4, 7) = ab$. With only one nonzero entry on the table, it would be difficult to speak of "peaking." Although we might consider that entry itself a "peak," there would still be no peaking in any column at $t = 3$, to reflect the perception of an ictus there. And there would be no peaking in the $d = 1$ column, reflecting the structuring role of that tactus for our metric impressions, particularly those at time point 3.

Intuitively, we would like a scanning function which, while having large spikes at time points 3 and 7, in the manner of (5.24), would also have smaller uniform spikes at time points 0, 1, 2, 5, 6, and 9, in the manner of (5.20) earlier. Such a function may be obtained mathematically by combining the function $g1$ of (5.20) with the function $g2$ of (5.24). The functions could be combined in a number of plausible ways. For instance, we could simply add $g2$, scaled by a suitable constant multiple C, to $g1$. This would give rise to a function of the form graphed in (5.25).

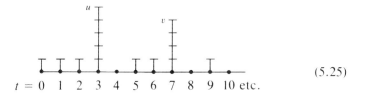

$$t = 0 \quad 1 \quad 2 \quad 3 \quad 4 \quad 5 \quad 6 \quad 7 \quad 8 \quad 9 \quad 10 \text{ etc.} \tag{5.25}$$

Here, supposing the short spikes to be of length 1, the longer spikes will be of lengths $u = 1 + aC$ and $v = 1 + bC$. This model interprets the "rhythmic accents" furnished by the rising-entropy model as being simply added on to the normal accents of the pulses at time points 3 and 7, to yield a scanning function.

We could also combine $g1$ and $g2$ so as to reflect a supposition that the role of "rhythmic accent" is rather to scale the proportional amount of importance we attach to each pulse. To obtain a "scaling function" $g3$, we could exponentiate $g2$: Fixing a suitable constant C greater than 1, we would take $g3(t) = C^{g2(t)}$, at each marked t. At all marked times other than $t = 3$ and 7, $g3(t)$ will then be equal to 1. (N.B. This is in particular the case for $t = 4$ and $t = 8$.) The values of $g3$ at times 3 and 7 will be, respectively, $u = C^a$ and $v = C^b$. Scaling $g1$ by multiplying it with $g3$, we would then again obtain a scanning function of the form graphed in (5.25).

The transformation of $g2$ to $g3$ is not far-fetched, considering that many of our acoustical perceptions vary logarithmically with respect to the measurements of the generating physical causes. Such perceptions as "pitch" and "loudness," for instance, must be exponentiated to obtain the respective corresponding physical "frequency" and "amplitude." Function $g3$ itself will not work as a scanning function because it takes on the value 1 at the time points 4 and 8. The unit spikes at $t = 4$ and $t = 8$ would give rise to unwanted W peaks at those times, as well as at $t = 3$ and 7. When we interpret $g3$ rather as scaling $g1$, that is, when we multiply the functions, the zero values for $g1$ at time points 4 and 8 give rise to zero values for the product function at those times.

A W table for the function of (5.25) is displayed in Table 5.6. The values in boldface will be the peaks, supposing that v, on (5.25), is greater than 2. Whatever model and scaling are used, that seems a reasonable supposition. Values of W for d greater than 5 are not computed.

A definitive explication for the problem under consideration is still far from being worked out: We have to decide, from among a number of plausible possibilities, just how we will assign H values to the marked time points; we will have to decide what method we want to use, in combining $g1$ and $g2$ (or $g1$ and $g3$, or perhaps yet other transforms of those functions) to obtain a scanning function; we will have to assign definite values to scaling constants (C, etc.) that may arise in the process of combination;

TABLE 5.6

$d =$	1	2	3	4	5
$t = 1$	1				
2	**2**	1			
3	**2 + u**	1 + u	u		
4	2 + u	1 + u	u		
5	2 + u	**1 + 2u**	1 + u	1	1
6	3 u	1 + 2u	1 + 2u	2	2
7	3 + u + v	1 + **2u** + v	1 + 2u	**2 + uv**	2 + v
8	3 + u + v	1 + 2u + v	1 + 2u	2 + uv	2 + v
9	3 + u + v	**1 + 2u + 2v**	2 + 2u	**3 + uv**	2 + v

etc. Still, I think the recent discussion does indicate how a rising-entropy model is of interest in considering how a rhythmic configuration in itself might "accent" certain pulses over others, even when all the individual pulses are acoustically indistinguishable.

We can rubato the stimulus of (5.20) a bit, using the continuous method to approximate that graph along the lines discussed at the beginning of the present Part. In that case, we would be "marking" not exact time points $t = 0, 1, 2, 3, 4, 5$, etc., but rather short time spans near and about those points. We would be expecting a possible pulse at some time during each marked time span. We would still measure H and H' discretely, from "mark" to "mark." The sense of the discussion would carry through; the mathematics would get too fussy to warrant its inclusion here.

Further Entropy-Related Models; Musical Syntax

My invocation of the word "entropy" may have reminded the reader of recent theoretical works that use the term, or kindred notions, in approaching rather broader grammatical or syntactical considerations of musical structure, including tonal structure.[18] As far as present matters

18. Leonard B. Meyer broke important ground in this respect (*Emotion and Meaning in Music* [Chicago: University of Chicago Press, 1956]). He used notions of expectation and uncertainty in an attempt to construct an ambitious theory along the lines of his title. Eugene Narmour reviews Meyer's later critique of that work, and adds his own criticisms (*Beyond Schenkerism: The Need for Alternatives in Music Analysis* [Chicago and London: The University of Chicago Press, 1977], pp. 136–41). Narmour attempts to develop an implication–realization model as an improvement. My approach here is quite foreign to that model, but Narmour does formulate perceptively, throughout his book, many methodological points about the relation of foreground processing to middle-ground structure that bear pointedly on my procedures. It is difficult for me to imagine how the systems of these theorists could

are concerned, I would care neither to associate myself with nor dissociate myself from any *Anschauung* that might be represented by such writings. My purpose, in invoking the idea here, has been only to aid in constructing exact numerical models specifically for our metric perception of small rhythmic structures in isolation. And the "uncertainty" involved has been more or less a matter of psychoacoustical common sense in the examples studied; I have not invoked, in particular, the conventions of any musical style.

To get a sense of how entropy-based models of the sort we have been considering might relate to local syntax, and to illustrate some of the techniques and pitfalls involved, it will be interesting to consider the widespread convention of modern Western musical thought that, in whatever style the distinctions are functional, strong beats are to carry consonances, and therefore dissonances are to appear on weak beats (or, perhaps more precisely, off strong beats.)[19]

We shall take it as given that there are substantially fewer ways of leaving a dissonance legally, in pertinent styles, than there are of leaving a consonance. We shall suppose further that these syntactic conventions are categorically prior to our metric impressions of a given passage in the style. (This is surely plausible at least as regards the listening process.) Now let us imagine, in some sort of second or third species situation, a succession of alternating consonances and dissonances at equally spaced time points 0, 1, 2, etc. (The regularity of this alternation, and of the rhythmic spacing, is not essential; it does, however, simplify the argument.) At each even-numbered time point, when we hear a state of consonance, we are relatively uncertain as to how the counterpoint will continue, since there are relatively many legal continuations. To clarify by oversimplifying, let us suppose there are N equally likely possibilities; our

---

easily lend themselves to the construction of synthetic numerical models; that is, such as would not attribute an indispensable function to an assumed common-practice style, as a statistical thesaurus in which a given musical composition is presumed to be embedded. In contrast, the approach of Iannis Xenakis is highly synthetic (*Formalized Music* [Bloomington and London: Indiana University Press, 1971]). Regardless of stylistic considerations, he believes that "sonic discourse is nothing but a perpetual fluctuation of entropy in all its forms" (*Formalized Music*, p. 76). Though he includes detailed and helpful explanations of his own compositional methods, he seems disinclined to plow through careful quantitative analyses of other, more neutral exemplary acoustical stimuli and musical passages. Accordingly, however one responds to his sweeping claim as an aesthetic credo, it cannot be said that he has put it on a theoretically solid objective basis.

19. The main apparent exception, the suspension dissonance, has generally been supposed by pertinent theorists for over five centuries to involve inter alia some sort of syncopation. It would be interesting to see if, and if so how, one might argue otherwise. But that is another story.

level of uncertainty, upon hearing a consonance, will then be measured by $H = \log N$. In contrast, at each odd-numbered time point, when we hear a state of dissonance, we are much less uncertain as to how the counterpoint will continue. Supposing there to be M equally likely continuations from the dissonance, our uncertainty will be measured by $H = \log M$. We are presuming that M is substantially less than N; their logarithms will then enjoy a similar relation. A graph for H values will resemble (5.26) below, whose tall spikes and short spikes are, respectively, of heights $\log N$ and $\log M$.

$$t = 0 \quad 1 \quad 2 \quad 3 \quad 4 \quad 5 \qquad \text{etc.} \qquad (5.26)$$

This figure has itself the form of the scanning function we intuitively want, and I would hypothesize that we should take H itself as such in this connection. For one thing, if we try to form H', we will have to choose between two models, as in the preceding section. Model 2, taking $H'(t) = H(t + 1) - H(t)$, puts positive H' values on the dissonances and negative values on the consonances. It will lead to a metric interpretation exactly the reverse of the one we want, so we shall reject it. Model 1, taking $H'(t) = H(t) - H(t - 1)$, attaches positive H' values to the consonances from $t = 2$ on, and negative values to the dissonances; it thus conforms better to our intuition. It seems hard to find any other reason for preferring model 1 to model 2 here, and it is hard to explain in particular why model 1 should be "right" here when model 2 was clearly "right" for the work of the preceding section. If we now continue, using model 1, we find that $H'(0)$ is not defined, since we can not meaningfully compare $H(0)$ to "$H(-1)$" in the model. If we chop off the negative values of H', we will get a function $g2$ that is not defined at time point 0, takes on zero values for odd-numbered time points, and takes on a constant positive value at each even-numbered time point from $t = 2$ on. This $g2$ would then have to be combined with some $g1$, in the manner of the preceding section, to arrive at something that would finally resemble (5.26) after all, only without the extended spike at time zero. Another drawback, for the $g2$ we have constructed, is that it will accent only consonance preceded by dissonance; it would take on zero values over all consonances beyond the first, in a succession of consonances. The H function of (5.26) accents all consonances more or less equally. In a context exhibiting long strings of successive consonances, it would predict decided loosening of any metric sense based on dissonance treatment, and corresponding susceptibility of the music to the cross-metric influence of accents in other dimensions, for example, rhythmic, registral, and textual. This prediction conforms well, to my hearing, with the effect of, say, the last phrase of Lassus's *Cantio duarum vocarum #1*, as regards the treatment of the half-notes.

To recapitulate: For the reasons just discussed, I should take the entropy function *H* graphed in (5.26) as a scanning function itself, rather than developing it further into a rising-entropy model. This methodology is, perplexingly, at odds with the procedures of the two previous sections, where the *H* function was clearly not satisfactory as a scanning function. Considering all the arguments adduced in the preceding sections, and the arguments just examined here, I would not care to override the discrepancy in the interests of an abstract "consistency," but it is puzzling. Perhaps it could be rationalized by the notion that we are here considering *H* as modeling disorganization in future (stylistic) expectation, whereas in the earlier work we were rather considering *H* as modeling disorganization in present (acoustical) perception, which then had to be "compared" with its future by constructing *H'*. It is terribly easy to slip into meaningless mumbo-jumbo, once one starts down such a metaphysical path, though.

One notes that the "stylistic accents" of (5.26) must be of considerable force, to override the opposite metric interpretation of the stimulus afforded by a purely psychoacoustic $f3/W3$ model along the lines of pages 121–127. For, supposing harmonically resonating sound sources, a dissonant stimulus will generally distribute energy over a wider band of frequencies than will a consonant one. (We must, as so often in such matters, finesse the problem of the "dissonant" perfect fourth here.) Perceived frequency-disorganization will therefore rise more sharply at a dissonant attack than at a consonant one. (If one voice does not change and the other moves stepwise, this sort of accent is minimized; if one voice sustains and the other leaps, as into various suspension dissonances, the accent is much greater.)

Summary and Concluding Remarks

Our fundamental construction has been the weighting function $W(d, t)$: This attributes a certain weight to duration *d* at time *t*, so as to produce metric interpretations of ictus at time *t*, and structural priority for duration *d* approaching time *t*, according to the peaking behavior of *W* at the pair (d, t).

The function $W(d, t)$ is always derived from a scanning function $f(t)$. Specifically, $W(d, t)$ is the sum or integral, over all pertinent values of $s \leq t$, of the individual products $f(s)f(s - d)$. The notion of "sum or integral'' here is susceptible to very powerful mathematical generalization. We could, for instance, accommodate scanning partly at discrete time points and partly over continuous time spans, or over even more pathological sets of time points.[20]

In our simplest model (Version 1), the scanning function f merely assumed a constant unit value over each member of a discrete set of time points. This enabled us to conceptualize W as a running temporal interval vector, updating a count of various durations as the time-point set unfolded through its own intrinsic chronology. Mathematically the simplest, this version of the theory is also the least problematical methodologically, to the extent it applies to a given situation. It seemed useful in connection with Bamberger's problem, and also in connection with some analytic observations on rhythmic aspects of a Schoenberg piece.[21]

We then attempted to extend the construction of the scanning function, to accomodate the possibility that certain time points might receive greater ''accent'' than others. These accents were to be represented by proportionally greater values for the scanning function at those times. A search for rational means of assigning specific numbers to those proportions led us to sophisticated and problematic considerations. The problems were minimal where the accents in question were purely dynamic, and perhaps maximal where the accents were purely rhythmic. Models involving variations in entropy, in one or more significant dimensions, seemed suggestive. But we did not succeed in finding a methodology for the construction of such models that was both uniformly consistent and in conformity with our intuition, over the various examples studied. Still, the speculative material of pages 121–136 does indicate a mode of thought through which the approach of pages 104–120 might eventually be extended consistently to deal with matters and problems on which it would otherwise have to remain uncomfortably silent.

20. For instance, although we would hardly wish to do so, we could avail ourselves of mathematical techniques that would enable us to scan over just those time points that could be expanded as infinite decimal numbers without using the digit 7.

21. A suggestive elaboration of this model is obtained by considering pairs (x, t), where x is a pitch or pitch class and t is a time point, say the point at which x is attacked. In that case, the interval pair (i, d) between the pairs (x, s) and (y, t) could be defined as the pair $(y - x, t - s)$. This pair models an occurrence of the pitch(-class) interval $i = y - x$ spanning the duration $d = t - s$ between the attack times of x and y. A discrete set of pairs of form (x, t) implies its own internal chronology, and hence can be ''unfolded'' in the sense of the present study, now in both pitch(-class) and time dimensions simultaneously. This gives rise to a running ''interval pair vector,'' which seems attractive both for theoretical and for analytical purposes. In the course of writing this paper, I recalled that I had in fact used just such a construction in an earlier paper (David Lewin, ''A Metrical Problem in Webern's Op. 27,'' *Journal of Music Theory*, vol. 6, no. 1, pp. 125–32). However, I no longer feel that my argument there is the best approach to examining the large metric structure of the movement at issue.

6

Charles J. Smith

PROLONGATIONS AND PROGRESSIONS AS MUSICAL SYNTAX

Musical analysts are concerned with making appropriate and interesting statements about pieces. No one, I imagine, would argue with such a claim; problems do arise, however, in its elaboration. The fact that someone finds a characterization of some piece appropriate or interesting does not guarantee that anyone else will as well. Certainly no general criteria for classifying analyses as appropriate or interesting can ever satisfy the intuitions of everyone. Yet neither property is completely indeterminate or totally subjective, for we often understand, or at least sympathize with, applications of the terms. I suspect that neither reflects any inherent property of analyses; rather appropriateness and interest are both properties of analyses *as perceived by particular musicians* with particular kinds of musical backgrounds. In other words, whether I think of an analysis as appropriate or interesting depends as much on the analytical strategies I am familiar with, the analyses I have done and read, and the pieces I know, as it does on the actual features of the analysis in question.

The pieces most of us know best are those we think of as tonal. The analyses that most clearly reflect opinions about appropriateness are those we develop in first getting to know tonal pieces. It is clear that Western musicians tend to apply only a few analytical strategies to most tonal pieces. We often focus on certain actual or abstracted sonorities as the essential underlying sounds ("chords"), while accounting for other sonorities as embellishments or transformations of chords. Then we isolate only certain successions of these chords, with leftover chords also thought of as embellishing a more essential succession. Focusing on chords in these ways is usually considered an appropriate approach to the so-called harmonic language of tonal pieces, on successions of chords an appropriate approach to musical directedness or coherence.

MUSIC THEORY: SPECIAL TOPICS

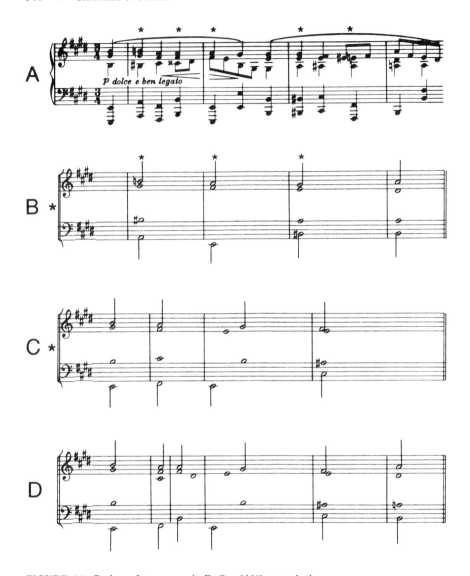

FIGURE 6.1. Brahms, Intermezzo in E, Op. 116/6, mm. 1–4.

Analyses, especially first analyses, that are built upon what would normally be thought of as embellishing sonorities will usually be considered
inappropriate. None of the starred sonorities in Figures 6.1A and 6.1B is
likely to be adopted as a chordal component of a first analysis of Brahms's
Op. 116/6; they will be thought of instead as variants of sonorities more

appropriately considered chords. Furthermore, a succession such as in Figure 6.1C, even though comprising legitimate chords, would not for most of us capture the harmonic direction of this passage; Figure 6.1D is more appropriate as part of an analytical first impression of a piece one expects to be straightforwardly tonal.

The question of analytical appropriateness becomes much fuzzier when characterizing tonal pieces in ways that less clearly reflect their tonality— for example, when discussing motivic patterns, or stepwise pitch connections without regard to any underlying harmonic framework. Some musicians may regard such characterizations as appropriate, but many will not. Confusion mounts further when dealing with music that is less obviously tonal; harmonic–function characterizations will usually be considered inappropriate for such pieces. Unfortunately, it can be difficult to find analyses of this music that will count as appropriate for anyone. Each of us may well know many pieces of which no appropriate characterizations have ever been enountered.

In any case, it seems clear that appropriateness cannot be aligned with mere truth. Even hopelessly misguided analyses rarely include any statements that are literally false. Our criticisms of poor analyses never treat of truth, except to identify inaccuracies. To criticize an analytical approach we say things like, ''I agree that these notes do occur in the order shown, but I question the value of characterizing them in such-and-such a way,'' or even, ''I question the value of isolating these particular notes for analytical attention.''

Nor is an accurate analysis ever inappropriate because it is incorrect in any sense. Figures 6.1B and 6.1C do display successions of sonorities that are peculiar when viewed from a traditional analytical perspective. But as characterizations can they be said to be wrong? Even the most far-fetched analysis could come to be viewed as appropriate, given enough exposure to similar characterizations. And, even if always thought of as inappropriate, such bizarre characterizations might eventually come to be considered interesting, especially with respect to the ways they complement more appropriate analyses.

If pinning down the sources of appropriateness is difficult, merely identifying the interesting components, if any, of a musical characterization is elusive. Are appropriate characterizations always interesting? (Surely not.) Are they ever? (Hard to say.) It may not even be possible to evaluate the interest of a given characterization without access to the complete piece and to a more comprehensive (and, at least in part, appropriate) analysis. Inappropriate analyses are not necessarily uninteresting; it is possible that, as Op. 116/6 becomes more familiar, the sonority successions of Figures 6.1B and 6.1C may assume more significance, may in fact reveal interesting things about that piece that cannot be shown in any more appropriate analysis. Even if no self-respecting Western musician would at first hearing focus on just those sonorities, is there not the potential for analytical mileage to be had from such apparent perversity?

In this chapter no distinction is made between appropriate or interesting analyses and the approaches or strategies by which they are arrived at, and for good reason. As already mentioned, our ascriptions of appropriateness and interest to analyses depend on our familiarity with the strategies we infer to lie behind the analyses. Noting this dependence resolves few questions, however, since it is unclear how one goes about identifying a strategy from an analysis, or if this is even possible. It is also unclear whether separate approaches to pieces can ever be said to manifest comparable, much less the same, strategies.

What follows is an attempt to formulate a systematic model for analytical strategies in general, turning them into what I call *syntaxes*. Discussion of analytical strategies is thus facilitated by reference to syntaxes, all of the same general structure. It also turns out that the systematizing of strategies serves more than a clarifying end, for the idea of *system* seems intimately related to that of appropriateness. I claim that appropriate characterizations are just those that reflect a position within a relatively secure syntax—which may or may not be familiar in an explicit formulation, of course. In other words, there are certain strategies–syntaxes that we habitually turn to in the initial stages of analytical discovery, because of their relatively well-supported position in our conceptual frameworks. Remarkably enough, all syntaxes, whether familiar or not, can be described in the same terms; there are no special formal features of the well-known strategies beyond their extrasystematic continued productivity.

On the other hand, interesting characterizations are not usually viewed as part of any established syntax, but they do exude the potential for generating new strategies. I suspect that even the most appropriate analyses are rarely perceived as wholly interesting by anyone. Rather, only certain features of any analysis are focused upon as interesting, that is, as pregnant with possibilities for further, systematic pursuit.

Prolongations—Vocabularies

In what follows I assume that pieces of music can be considered sequences of of irreducible *events*—what we would casually refer to in most pieces as the notes. Every such event will be assumed to have an easily specified initiation or attack point. (End points are often harder to locate; they usually depend on the sorts of prolongations an event is heard as contributing to.) In most pieces there will be many mutually overlapping events. A *sonority* at some time is the set of all events begun at or before that time and not yet ended.

It is useful to focus on the *isolation* of a set of events and the *characterization* of that set as two distinguishable components of any analytical observation. Statements of isolation will count as relatively observational for those who are conversant with the notational system being used. Characterizations count as less observational, that is, as dependent on collateral information which can only be expressed in nonobservational, theoretical statements.[1]

Essentially there are only two ways to isolate a set of events. We can specify a continuous *segment* of a piece, by picking out beginning and ending times. Only well-behaved segments are recognized here, those whose beginnings and endings correspond to the attacks of some events. Even in such considerate cases, events often extend over the boundaries between neighboring segments.

Alternatively, we can specify a *subsequence* of a piece, a series of not necessarily adjacent events. If any two events in such a series are simultaneously attacked, then it is usually convenient to regard them as parts of a compound event that occupies just one slot in the subsequence; in other cases, events can be considered to be ordered by their attack times. One particular type of analytical subsequencing performed upon many pieces, that is, a slicing into distinct *lines*, is especially important in discussions of voice-leading and nonchord tones. Of course, deciding to isolate a subsequence in an analysis does not entail considering that subsequence a line.

Even these two apparently distinct analytical maneuvers turn out to be interdependent.[2] Picking out a subsequence delineates a series of contiguous segments, each initiated by the attack of an event in the sequence. (Going from segments to subsequences is trickier, but still possible.) This chapter focuses on the problems encountered in characterizing segments; an extension to subsequences is straightforward.

Any *leveled* structure can be thought of either as several nested subsequences or as several nested segmentations. When dealing with an analysis containing several different segmentations of the same passage, we can identify segmentations as being on a similar *level* or of comparable *scope* if they divide the passage in question into approximately the same number of segments; one segmentation is of greater scope or on a higher

---

1. See W. V. Quine, *Word and Object* (Cambridge, Massachusetts: MIT Press, 1960), pp. 26–57.

2. For more detail on this dependency, see my "Rhythm Restratified," *Perspectives of New Music* 16/1 (Fall–Winter 1977), pp. 155–60.

level than another if it has significantly fewer segments in the same passages.

Once isolated, a segment of a piece can be characterized trivially by listing some or all of its constituent events, or by providing a breakdown into smaller segments. Fortunately, musical characterization is not wholly a trivial matter, as there is an alternative analytical maneuver available, a maneuver that is an essential part of all substantial musical thought. An entire segment, of whatever length, can be characterized as a single manifestation of some discrete thing. I will refer to a segment so characterized as a *prolongation;*[3] if that segment is heard as an X, then it is said to be a prolongation of X.

Given any segment to be heard as a prolongation, two sets of questions must be dealt with more or less separately:

1. What sort of thing will this segment be heard as? Will it be heard as a chord, a motivic figure, a formal component or section, a single pitch(-class), or something else entirely? What kinds of chords, motives, etc., can be chosen from?
2. What specific thing of this sort will the segment be heard as—*which* chord, *which* motive, etc.?

To characterize in terms of prolongations, we must search through various *vocabularies* or repertories of things-to-be-heard-in-pieces, picking a listing of prolongable things, as well as deciding upon the specific prolongations to be heard. An examination of an analytical characterization must deal not only with the actual segmentations and prolongations asserted, but also with the prolongation vocabularies that were sifted through by the analyst along the way—to whatever extent these can be reconstructed or hypothesized.

Prolongations do not necessarily contain a literal manifestation of the thing prolonged. In certain kinds of prolongations the thing prolonged is not even comparable to any set of events contained in the segments in question. Common examples are found in almost any discussion of so-called musical form. Segments are delineated (sometimes very loosely) and characterized by choosing terms from a large vocabulary that includes such things as "A," "second-theme group," "trio," and "double period." None of these things is ever encountered except as a prolongation; the terms involved are only used to describe segments. A segment

---

3. The point of using a term borrowed from tonal theory is to emphasize that what we normally think of as chord prolongations are but one example of a general analytical phenomenon.

might be heard as a prolongation of a chord or a motive that it also contains, but no segment can be heard both to be and to contain a recapitulation.[4]

Assuming that the thing prolonged in a segment is conceivable as a set of events and hence as potentially comparable to something contained in that segment, there are two distinct possibilities to consider:

1. The thing prolonged is a sequence of successive events—a *horizontal* prolongation.
2. The thing prolonged is a set of events with simultaneous attacks—a *vertical* prolongation.

Any actual manifestations of these prolonged things need not be successive or simultaneously respectively. A simultaneity can be heard as a vertical manifestation of a sequence (see Figure 6.4B), and a sequence can be heard as an arpeggiation of a simultaneity (Figure 6.7C, p. 152).

The prototypical horizontal prolongations involve what we usually refer to as *motivic figures;* the shapes to be recognized depend on the prolongation vocabulary selected for a particular sketch. In Figure 6.2, the beginning of Brahms's Op. 116/6 is represented in terms of prolongations of (E major) diatonic scale patterns of varying length, in Figure 6.3 as chromatic or diatonic scale patterns, and in Figure 6.4 as parallel scale patterns in 3rds, 4ths, 5ths, and 6ths.[5] Obviously, Figure 6.2 can be heard as closely related to, even derived from, both Figures 6.3 and 6.4, but it can also be considered a distinct analysis, representing an aspect of this passage not directly revealed by either alternative. Figure 6.5 exhibits a different kind of motivic figure; every prolongation shown is a three-event cambiata with intervals of various sizes. As is often the case in motivic analyses, the first such figure, containing a 4th and a 3rd, is the prototype for the rest of the sketch.

There is clearly a great deal of room for creativity in the development of motivic vocabularies; we are free to specify (or not to specify) the number of events, directional configuration and relative interval sizes, the pitch universe inhabited (whether chromatic, diatonic, triadic, or some other collection of pitches), the allowable intervals from that universe, and the

4. The term "recapitulation" is comparable to such things as "prolongation of V" or "prolongation of an E–F-sharp–E neighbor figure." When we talk of sets of events contained within segments, we use labels like "V" or "E–F-sharp–E neighbor"; there are no such terms for formal things, no way of talking about recapitulations with the implicit "prolongation of . . ." removed.

5. To save space, several motive prolongations are shown in most segments of these sketches.

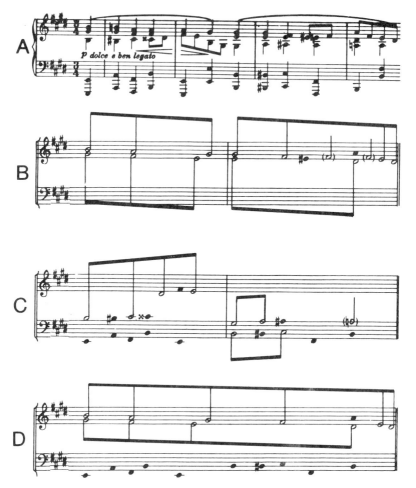

FIGURE 6.2. Brahms, Intermezzo in E, Op. 116/6 mm. 1–4.

Vocabulary: (E major) diatonic scale figures, any length

Notation: ♪♪♪ (♩) = prolonged figure (with repetitions)
            | | = segment/prolongation
            •   = residue

extent of the equivalence produced by octave (or some other interval) transposition. Figure 6.6 exhibits two different kinds of three-event neighbor-note figures, the first within an E-major diatonic universe, the second within a triadic universe; both sketches show only adjacent neighbor notes within their respective universes, and both allow octave-related events a certain degree of equivalence (at least in the bass register).

FIGURE 6.3. Brahms, Intermezzo in E, Op. 116/6, mm. 1–4.
Vocabulary: chromatic/diatonic scale figures, any length

Representing a passage as a number of prolongations based on one vocabulary member entails that all the prolonged segments can be heard as
comparable, since they are all characterized as prolongations of "the
same thing." In fact, the more general a conception of some figure is, the
more likely that all configurations can be made to appear comparable.
However, unqualified assertions of identity are not very helpful in developing persuasive characterizations of music. Broadly based analyses are
enhanced if balanced against other, less inclusive sketches; Figures 6.3
and 6.4 are most effective if read in conjunction with Figure 6.2. Furthermore, even when dealing with a single analysis, a process of differentiation can follow the transformation of segments into prolongations; we aim
at presenting a particular segment as a particular prolongation of some
thing, and not just as one more undistinguished version of it. This sort of
differentiation is carried out by focusing on two distinct aspects of any
prolongation. We can *describe* the particulars of presentation of the prolonged thing in that segment (if it is presented at all). Alternatively, we
can talk about the events that do not take part in any manifestation of the
thing prolonged—the *residue* or leftovers of the prolongation.

Describing motivic prolongations involves speaking of a number of
things: How much of a segment is exhausted by the prolonged motive? Do
motives and segments begin and end together? We usually confine motivic

FIGURE 6.4. Brahms, Intermezzo in E, Op. 116/6, mm. 1–4.
Vocabulary: alternating-scale figures, in parallel 3rds, 4ths, 5ths, or 6ths

prolongations to segments immediately enclosing them, as in Figure 6.5. This correlation is so strong that two figures that are not simultaneous throughout but that begin and end together will often be heard as equivalent, if in a loose sense (for example, Figure 6.3, B to E and G-sharp to E). But longer segments can also reasonably be heard as prolongations of shorter motives. In Figures 6.2, 6.3, 6.4, and 6.6, most of the prolonga-

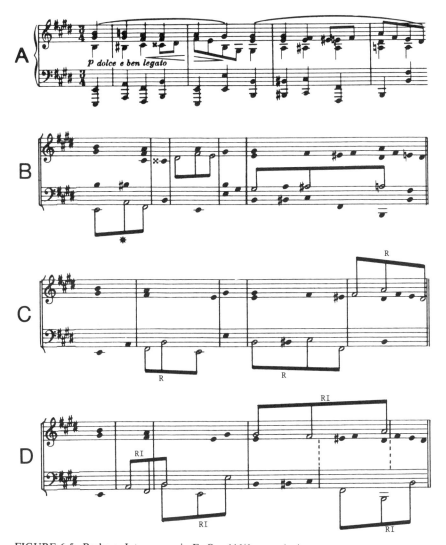

FIGURE 6.5. Brahms, Intermezzo in E, Op. 116/6, mm. 1–4.

   Vocabulary: three-event cambiata figures (two intervals, different directions, one larger than the other), any intervals, any contour

   Notation: * = prototype figure
             R = reverse of the prototype with respect to contour
             I = inverse of the prototype

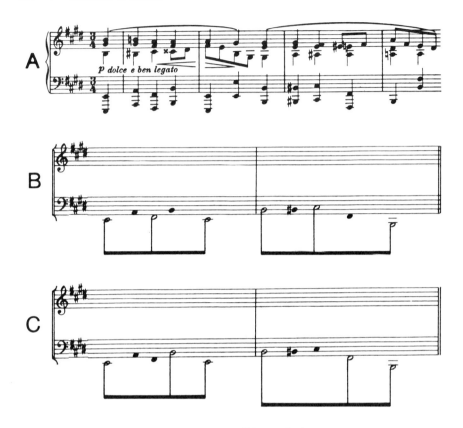

FIGURE 6.6. Brahms, Intermezzo in E, Op. 116/6, mm. 1–4.
Vocabulary: three-event neighbor figures, with respect to (B) diatonic universe, (C) triadic universe.

tions shown are over two segments—what would normally be identified, for harmonic and other reasons, as the "phrases" of the passage—despite the fact that many of the motives prolonged do not exhaust these segments.

Are the segments in a sketch contiguous? Do they overlap? Do the prolonged motives overlap? Unlike Figures 6.2–6.4, Figure 6.5 is intended to emphasize overlap and discontinuity between segments; Figure 6.5D exhibits two different ways of representing overlapping motives. What pitches, if any, do comparable motives share (B–B-sharp–C sharp and G-sharp–A in Figure 6.3, for example)? Are portions of any motives repeated or elaborated upon (F-sharp–D-sharp in Figure 6.4B). Do harmonic patterns support motivic patterns in any way; specifically, which events in which motives are chord-tones with respect to which chord prolongations (as discussed below)? Not surprisingly, harmonic considerations often affect our choice of motivic figures; E-sharp is not included in the upper voice of Figure 6.3 only because it is difficult to hear as a chord tone or as doing anything other than elaborating F-sharp.

It is not as clear how to deal with the residue of a motivic prolongation. While the leftovers of a vertical prolongation are usually characterized in horizontal terms (see page 154), as belonging to lines of some sort, motivic leftovers are not easy to fit into subsidiary vertical patterns. We usually talk of the residue in a motivic prolongation horizontally, if at all; leftover events comprise other motivic manifestations, which for the purposes of that sketch are subordinate to the prolonged motives. It is conceivable that some events in a motivic residue could be characterized in vertical terms—if, for example, a motivic figure is decorated with or interrupted by an arpeggiation of some chord. Thus, in Figures 6.2B and 6.2D, the soprano A in m. 4 can be heard as a chord-derived event, embellishing the prolonged scale figures.

Vertical prolongations are more familiar and natural to most Western musicians, since the set of diatonic triadic *chords* constitutes the prolongational vocabulary we know best. As with horizontal prolongations, the selection of a vocabulary is of fundamental importance to an analysis, whose principal reflection is of the vocabulary chosen. In this section, I shall deal only with the usual set of "functional" chords, identified in what I hope is a noncontroversial way. It should not be assumed that these chords, despite the readiness with which we invoke them and teach them (under the rubric of "tonality"), constitute a completely well-determined vocabulary shared by all. We each have our separate notions about which of the many refinements of harmonic theory to accept as prolongable chords; the debate rages still over ninth, eleventh, and thirteenth chords, chromatic mediants, and half-diminished seventh chords on the dominant, to cite a few questionable entries.

Figure 6.7 presents four alternative chord-prolongational views of the beginning of Op. 116/6. A comparison of 6.7D and 6.7E reveals the effect that our almost instinctive formal segmentations can have on judgments about chord prolongations. Figure 6.7D reflects a phrase segmentation we would all presumably agree with, and which is in fact notated in the score (Figure 6.7A). Figure 6.7E seems a less reasonable presentation of chords, but only because the blurring over of this phrase division might make us uneasy. Similarly, in Figures 6.7B and 6.7C, we may well be tempted to reflect this phrase division more clearly by considering the I and the I_4^6 as separate chord prolongations—hence the dotted bar lines. Of course, formal segmentations cannot be treated as the unquestioned "given" of music, not even of tonal music; we can only hear a segment as

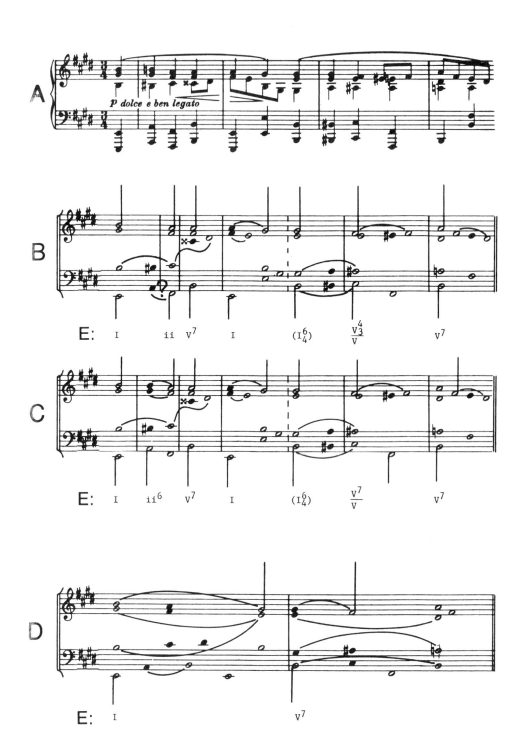

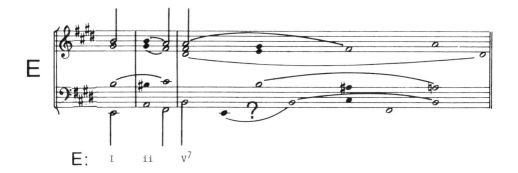

FIGURE 6.7. Brahms, Intermezzo in E, Op. 116/6, mm. 1–4.
Vocabulary: diatonic triads and seventh chords from E (and B)

Notation: = outer voices of prolonged chord

= nonchord tone in some linear configuration
= a debatable segmentation

a "phrase" prolongation if harmonic and other patterns coincide to some extent, that is, if patterns such as that in Figure 6.7D turn out to be persuasive.

The description of vertical prolongations begins, as does that of horizontal prolongations, with the relation between segments and the things prolonged and contained therein. Because chords are normally conceived as simultaneities, a prolongation of a chord usually begins with the attack of that chord and not before. However, the attack of a chord may not be easy to locate; is the ii chord in m. 1 attacked as in Figures 6.7B or C? In such cases, we often let the bass cue the entrance of the chord, as in Figure 6.7C, a predisposition resulting from certain kinds of theoretical training. There is also a strong tendency, other things being equal, to let chord-prolongation segmentations coincide with metrical segmentations as much as possible; again Figure 6.7C wins over 6.7B. Of course, other things are rarely equal; we usually regard metrical segmentations as viable only if they correspond to some extent with chordal segmentations.

Some segments begin and end with the prolonged chord (e.g., Figure 6.7D, first segment); others begin with a clear manifestation of their contained chords, but end with sonorities which are more or less different (Figure 6.7B, first segment). The former might be called *continuations,* the latter *protractions,* but this is at most a relative distinction. If a chord makes a straggled entrance, there may never be any sonority that is a direct manifestation of the prolonged chord. However, if there are several manifestations in some segment, it may be useful to talk about the extent to which they *match* each other.

In describing the chordal events themselves, it is often productive, as the notation of Figure 6.7 suggests, to focus on just one pair of outer voice ("soprano" and "bass") events for each prolongation. If it is difficult to pick out just one soprano or bass event from among several options, the "best" solution may be to show the alternatives in separate sketches; compare the bass in Figures 6.7B and C, fifth segments, and the soprano in Figures 6.7B and C, sixth segments. The choice of outer voices is often dependent on the sort of progressions heard and how those progressions are to be described—matters for the next section of this chapter.

The residue of chord prolongations consists of *nonchord tones* of various sorts. It is usual to distinguish between *accented* and *unaccented* nonchord tones, but there are two different ways of doing this. "Accented" can mean "occurring at the beginning of a metrical segment (a measure, a half-measure, etc.)"; however, in this chapter, "accented (with respect to a prolongation)" means "occurring as part of the first sonority of that prolongation." According to this latter usage, A and B-sharp are unaccented nonchord tones in the first prolongation of Figure 6.7B, but B-sharp is an accented nonchord tone in Figure 6.7C. Of course, A is a chord tone in Figure 6.7C. Status as a nonchord tone is not an absolute property of any musical event; rather, how an event is heard depends on the prolongations being heard around it.

We usually try to hear nonchord tones in horizontal terms, that is, as belonging to certain standardized linear figures—hence the traditional names "passing note," "neighbor note," "cambiata," etc. In fact, the ease with which we can force the nonchord tones in some prolongation through these traditional filters is one measure of how persuasive that prolongation will be—another reason for preferring Figure 6.7C to 6.7B.

Any prolongation which contains nonchord tones also contains *nonchord sonorities*. A nonchord sonority might be referred to as a *linear chord* if most of its component nonchord tones, especially those in the outer voices, can be heard as standard linear configurations. Thus the first sonority of the second prolongation of Figure 6.7C is a nonchord sonority; since the G-sharp and B can be heard as suspensions and the B-sharp as an accented (chromatic) passing note, this sonority could be characterized as a linear chord, or, more specifically, as a suspension–appoggiatura chord. The only sonority of the second prolongation of Figure 6.7B is, of course, a chord sonority there, but in Figure 6.7D it is a nonchord sonority, specifically a linear (passing) chord. Once again, it is meaningless to characterize most sonorities as nonchord sonorities or as linear chords *without first specifying the prolongation(s) with respect to which they are so heard.*

Some sonorities turn out to be nonchord sonorities not just with respect to individual prolongations but with respect to an entire vocabulary. The A–B-sharp–G-sharp–B sonority in m. 1 of Op. 116/6 is a nonchord sonority in all prolongations based on traditional diatonic triadic chords; this sonority can never be heard as a direct manifestation of one of those chords. A nonchord sonority with respect to a prolongation is not necessarily a nonchord sonority with respect to the vocabulary utilized, of course. However, a nonchord sonority with respect to some vocabulary must be a nonchord sonority with respect to any prolongation based on that vocabulary.

Even though a segment of prolongation has been determined, it may not be clear *which* chord is to be prolonged there—that is, which component events are chord tones and which are to accounted for as residue. In Figure 6.8, two versions of m. 6 of Chopin's Op. 25/12 are offered. Neither seems exclusively correct; in fact, neither is altogether convincing by

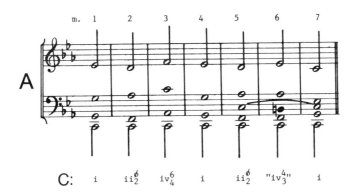

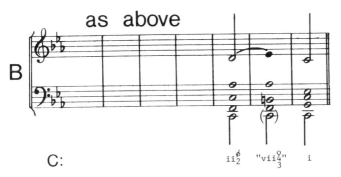

FIGURE 6.8. Chopin, Etude in C minor, Op. 25/12, mm. 1–7.
    Vocabulary: diatonic triads and seventh chords from C (minor)
    Notation: (♩) = bass nonchord tone (pedal)

itself. It is difficult to account for B as a nonchord tone in Figure 6.8A and the voice leading (see page 161) of Figure 6.8B is peculiar. What is clear is that this measure can be heard as a prolongation both of iv and of vii°. Characterizing it as only one or the other inevitably lessens the impact of the passage.

There is no good reason to assume that only one persuasive prolongational view of any piece exists, or only one set of nested prolongations—even with respect to a single vocabulary. Furthermore, my focusing exclusively on a familiar chord vocabulary is not meant to imply that these chords make up the only viable vertical prolongations. Given any piece, there may well be a large number of familiar and not-so-familiar vocabularies that can be utilized in segmenting and prolonging. Given any segment, adoption of different vocabularies may lead to the construction of alternative, equally persuasive prolongations over that segment.

This seems to be the essence of characterization in terms of prolongations. We strive to hear complex passages as relatively simple, regular things, to characterize relatively opaque things in terms of containing prolongations, and to hear things which at first seem incomparable as rewrites of one another. In the process we develop rich characterizations of complex music from relatively simple theoretical bases, by focusing on the interaction of different prolongational accounts of the same passage, rather than on the mere labeling from one point of view.

Progressions—Orderings

Dissection of the prolongational structure of analyses is a helpful first step in a discussion of appropriateness and interest, but matters are far from resolved. For unfortunately Figure 6.1C makes as much sense from the chord-prolongational point of view as does Figure 6.1D; yet 6.1D seems much more appropriate.

What is needed is a characterization of the analytical process which treats Figure 6.1D as a *functional progression*[6] and Figure 6.1C not. But first a word of warning: Any such process cannot be said to operate only *after* the construction of the prolongations in question. That an outline of an analytical approach (as here) presents X before Y or defines Y in terms of X does not mean that X and Y are successive or even wholly separable operations. An order of presentation does not entail a corresponding order of application; what is suggested is only a convenient way of look-

---

6. Like "prolongation," the term "progression" has its origin in tonal theory, but the use made of it here is more general.

ing at things. It would be impossible even to sort out and notate events in any piece, much less to construct prolongations, without powerful long-range assumptions about the sorts of progressions we expect to be able to find; without such expectations, analytical thought is comparatively impoverished on all levels. Thus, in Op. 116/6, if we regard one event in m. 1 as Cx and acquiesce to its being labeled as such, this is because we are primarily interested in hearing a dominant seventh chord rather than a minor seventh chord; we want that chord because we are looking for a certain succession of chord prolongations; and we aim for that succession because we are trying to hear Op. 116/6 as a tonal piece.

My concern in this section is with the fact that, given a number of ways to hear successions of prolongations in a piece, we usually consider certain successions more appropriate than others. A sophisticated and systematic prolongation vocabulary is likely to be accompanied by a *progression system,* a listing in some form of those successions that are acceptable as *progressions.* A progression can be thought of as a *well-formed* succession of prolongations, that is, as a particular *ordering* of prolongations which is singled out for analytical attention.

A progression system is essentially a predetermination of those successions that will be allowed to count as progressions. Only the recognition of a prior decision to hear certain patterns in a piece can account for the sense of directedness and culmination when those patterns are actually heard. That some progression systems (one in particular!) are thoroughly entrenched in our analytical habits is a result not so much of innate correctness or natural supremacy; we can only observe that for now some systems manage to reward their application more richly than do others.

The basic notion underlying musical progression is that of *functionality.* Progressions within elaborate prolongation vocabularies are often constructed upon *functional categories.*[7] Not every prolongable thing will necessarily be subsumed into some functional category; some things may be contained in more than one category; in some vocabularies every prolongable thing may constitute a separate category. But in general each member of a prolongation vocabulary will be assigned one of a few functional labels.

The best-known examples of progression systems are those with which we amplify our notions of vertical (chord) prolongations in tonal pieces. The tonal–functional system outlined here is deliberately primitive; func-

7. This term is adapted from the categorical grammar for language devised by K. Adjukiewicz, in "On Syntactical Coherence," *Review of Metaphysics* 20/4 (No. 80, June 1967), pp. 635–47 (an article originally published in German in *Studia philosophica* of 1935).

tional categories are narrow and allowable progressions are few. Because of these minimal assumptions, relatively few musical passages will count as tonal progressions—both a strength and a weakness of this sort of approach. It is unavoidable, even desirable, that other musicians will want to develop different systems, if only because some pieces seem to demand different systems. But the following is easily amended or edited.[8]

Any tonal–functional system will be built upon a 12-pitch-class universe (that is, with some limited form of octave equivalence) that contains a diatonic pitch collection and its transpositions. This collection will be thought of as containing a triad and its transpositions, each with one pitch as root; the root of one triad is thought of as the tonic or key of the whole diatonic collection as well.[9] I will regard the modes, especially major and minor, as different colorings of the same key, rather than as separate tonalities; there are therefore only 12 distinguishable keys.

All tonal expeditions must be embarked upon with a particular key in mind; talk of tonal function is empty without reference to some tonic. In cases where it is unclear which is the key of a piece, several such expeditions may be called for, each from a different point of view; these separate characterizations will inevitably contribute to each other's success.

The three functional categories to be used here are *tonic* (T), *dominant* (D), and *dominant preparation* (DP).[10] Table 6.1 lists a basic chord-prolongation vocabulary grouped into these three categories. The further division into primary, substitute, and chromatic subcategories reflects a hierarchy that is more stylistic than functional. (The details of added sevenths and chord-inversional identity present technical problems of formulation rather than conceptual difficulties, and are omitted here.)

A succession of chord prolongations is said to be a *chord progression* if it is a succession of four prolongations, belonging to the functional categories T, DP, D, and T, respectively. This succession T–DP–D–T can be referred to as a *progression paradigm.*

Certain *transformations* of this paradigmatic progression must be allowed.

T1. Duplication: Two or more chords from the same functional category may occupy any slot in a paradigm. (Sometimes these adjacent chords can be considered a single composite prolongation.)

8. A different approach to the same sort of tonal progression system is worked out by Marion A. Guck in "The Functional Relations of Chords: A Theory of Musical Intuitions," *In Theory Only* 4/6 (November–December 1978), pp. 29–42.

9. See William E. Benjamin, "Tonality without Fifths," *In Theory Only* 3/2 (May 1977), p. 17.

10. These categories date back at least to Riemann's tonic, dominant, and subdominant.

TABLE 6.1
Functional Categories for Tonal Chord Prolongations

Category	Tonic (T)	Dominant (D)	Dominant preparation (DP)
Primary	I (i)^a	V	ii (ii^0) IV (iv) vi (bVI)
Substitute (S)	vi (bVI) [iii (bIII)]?	vii^0	iii (bIII)
Chromatic substitute (C)	$\dfrac{V^7}{IV} \dfrac{V^7}{iv}$ $\dfrac{V^7}{V}, \dfrac{vii^0_7}{V}$ $\dfrac{vii^0_7}{ii}$ and many others, all of which will be notated as "I" ("i")	V$^+$	bII Augmented 6th chords: It6, Fr6, Ger6

^{a} Parentheses indicate minor mode correlate if different from major mode.

T2. Substitution: In any functional slot, a substitute or chromatic chord may appear instead of a primary—notated TS, DPS, DS, TC, DPC, or DC. (For stylistic reasons we would, of course, be surprised to find such chords in some places, such as at the ends of pieces.)

T3. Omission: The DP functional slot may be omitted altogether.

T4. Truncation: A progression may lack an initial or a final T functional slot. (If this "or" is interpreted as inclusive rather than exclusive, then, in light of (T3), a single D prolongation could count as a progression.)[11]

---

11. In an alternative formulation, based on Adjukiewicz's categorical grammar, the basic categories are P (for progression) and T (tonic). The two most important functorial categories are D and DP, which can be defined as follows:

$$D = \xleftrightarrow[T,T]{P} \qquad \text{(something that yields P when surrounded by T's)}$$

$$DP = \dfrac{\xleftrightarrow[T,T]{P}}{\xleftrightarrow[T,T]{P}} \qquad \text{(something that yields D when placed before a D)}$$

Transformation (T3) is now superfluous. (T4) necessitates two additional subcategories:

$$D' = \xleftarrow{P}{T} \qquad \text{and} \qquad D'' = \xrightarrow{P}{T}$$

Adjacent progressions can either share tonics or have different tonics. In the former case, there is only one mode of *combination*.

C1. Concatenation, which allows configurations like:

$$\underline{\text{T} - \text{DP} - \text{D} - \text{T}_|} - \text{D} - \text{T}$$

With respect to different keys, there are two possibilities.

C2. Insertion, which allows configurations like (with respect to keys X and Y):

X: T – DP –   – D – T

Y: T – D – T

and

X: T –   – DP – D – T

Y: – DP – D – T

C3. Reinterpretation, which allows configurations like:

X: T – DP –

Y: – DP – D – T

and

X: T – DP – D –

Y: – DP – D – T

and

X: T – DP –

Y: T – D – T

Similar combinations and transformations can be developed for progressions of other sorts of prolongations. With respect to tonal chords, insertion is traditionally referred to as tonicization, reinterpretation as modulation. The difference between the two is relative, and has to do with the level or scope of the progressions under consideration; when given passages are heard in terms of segmentations of greater scope, reinterpretations are often transformed into insertions, and insertions into single chords.

These guidelines can be summed up as follows:

T   can be followed by a T, a DP, or a D in any key.

DP can be followed by another DP, by a D, or by an inserted progression, or can be reinterpreted in another key.

D can be followed by another D, by a T, or by an inserted progression, or can be reinterpreted in another key, or can be the end of a truncated progression (as at a half-cadence), and thus can be followed by anything.

All other successions of chord prolongations can be heard only as successions, not as progressions, at least not with respect to this system.

Figure 6.9 exhibits a few of the many chord prolongations which can be heard in the first 49 measures of Chopin's Op. 10/1; Figure 6.9A is an octave-equivalence reduction of this passage to a succession of four-voice chords, upon which succession the other two sketches are based. Functional categories are indicated, and progressions are bracketed beneath the traditional Roman numerals. The assignment of categories can produce anomalies; here, for example, the chord in m. 33 (see Figure 6.9A) can reasonably be heard as a tonic, as a dominant, and as a dominant preparation, with respect to three different keys.

The description of chord progressions has to do with what we traditionally call *voice leading*. We normally try to find lines which are for the most part stepwise and composed of one event from each chord examined. These linear patterns are directly comparable with those manifested by the nonchord tones in persuasive chord prolongations; in fact, the voice-leading pattern of some progression often turns out to be the nonchord tone pattern of a higher-level prolongation found in the same passage (e.g., the soprano of mm. 1–9 in Figures 6.9B and C).[12]

The residue of a progression on a certain level consists of prolongations of chords on any lower level that do not figure in that progression. These chords can be referred to as *nonfunctional chords* with respect to that progression. (If some chord is part of no progressions at all, even though a viable prolongation of a bona fide vocabulary member, then it can be said to be nonfunctional with respect to the progression system as a whole.) For example, the third chord of Figure 6.9A is functional on that level but nonfunctional with respect to the progressions of Figure 6.9B and D; it is also a nonchord sonority with respect to the prolongations containing it on each of these three levels, in fact, as shown in Figure 6.9B, a linear (passing) chord. Any nonfunctional chord with respect to some progression is a nonchord sonority with respect to the prolongation in that progression which contains it; the converse is not usually true, of course. As with nonchord tones and sonorities, a chord can only be said to be

12. Schenker was the first theorist to stress that the same sorts of voice-leading patterns can be found in large-scale and small-scale chord progressions, and that low-level progressions are often persuasively regarded as comprising linear elaborations of prolongations of larger scope.

162

FIGURE 6.9. (Legend on p. 164)

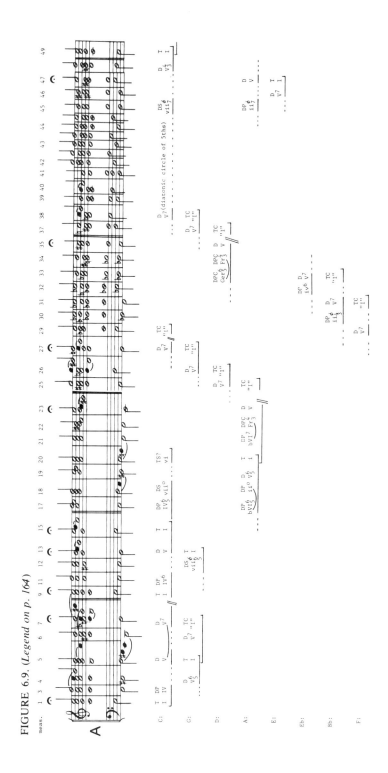

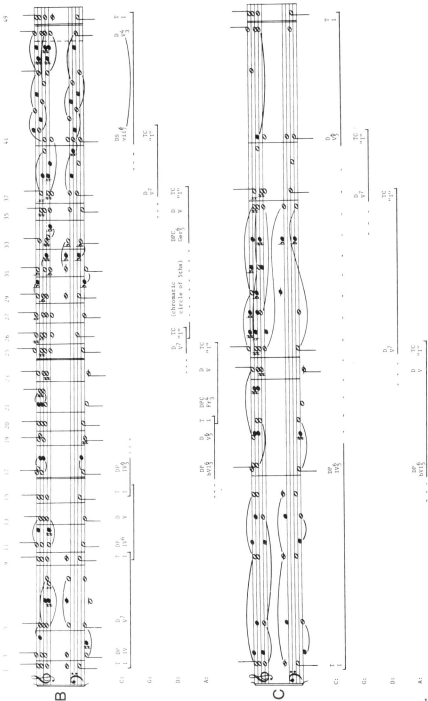

163

nonfunctional with respect to a particular progression. Functional qualifications are relative, not absolute.

This chord-progression system is so intimately bound up with our identification of certain pieces as "tonal" (as well as with our sense of what constitutes appropriate analyses of them) that a formulation of the connection seems in order. Someone hears a piece as *tonal* if (and only if?) he hears that piece for the most part as progressions of triadic chord prolongations, as already outlined; some of these progressions will usually be of large enough scope to subsume almost the entire piece. We cannot require that there be only one way on each level of slicing a piece up into prolongations and progressions; there are often many equally persuasive ways (see Figures 6.11C and C'). Nor can we require that every sonority be hearable as part of a prolongation or that every prolongation be part of some progression; such is not the case in the most straightforward cases. In fact, the issue here is not whether a piece *is* tonal or what *can* be heard in it in any absolute sense, however much we may like to speak in these terms; what matters is the *point of view* from which a piece is heard and *what* actually is heard thereby. Those pieces we casually describe as "tonal" are just those we believe or assume to be appropriately characterized from this particular "tonal" perspective. When we speak of what can be heard in a piece, we address a similar belief, namely that along these lines lies a productive analysis.

Despite our allegiance to this tonal system, different chord progression systems, using the same chord vocabulary, can be devised. Table 6.2 outlines what might be described as a *plagal* system, which, though not as fertile as the tonal system, is obviously applicable to many ostensibly tonal pieces.[13]

---

13. Just as the essential part of any tonal progression can be considered to be T–D–T, with its implicit lines $\hat{1}-\hat{7}-\hat{1}$ and $\hat{3}-\hat{4}-\hat{3}$, the essence of a plagal progression seems to be T–P–T, with a common-tone rather than a half-step line, $\hat{1}-\hat{1}-\hat{1}$.

FIGURE 6.9. Chopin, Etude in C, Op. 10/1, mm. 1–49.

    Vocabulary: diatonic triads and 7th chords from C and other keys
    Functional categories: T, DP, D
    Progression paradigm: T – DP – D – T (as outlined above)
    Notation:

                    = complete progression
                    = beginning-truncated progression
                    = interrupted progression
                    = end-truncated progression (at half-cadence)
                    = end-truncated progression (reinterpreted)
                    = connects Roman numerals of the same functional
                        category
                    = phrase boundary
                    = chords of more than 1 m. duration

TABLE 6.2
A Plagal Chord Progression System[a,b]

Category	Tonic (T)	Plagal (P)	Plagal preparation (PP)
Primary	I (i)	IV (iv)	iii (bIII) V (v) vii⁰ (bVII)
Substitute		ii⁷ (ii♯) vi (bVI)	
Chromatic substitute		Augmented 6th chords #ii₇⁰ and many others	

[a] Plagal progression paradigm: T–(PP)–P–T.
[b] Transformations and combinations: (as outlined above).

Other systems can be built upon, among other possibilities, tonally bizarre "resolutions" of familiar chords, or successions of what would normally be regarded as nonchord sonorities. Chopin's Op. 10/1 can be productively heard in terms of the two-chord progression which would be traditionally notated V/vi–V. Every root position V/vi in this piece is eventually followed by V, first (mm. 23–28) in a straightforward tonal context, but then (mm. 47–48 and 65–68) in two passages that are relatively anomalous in any tonal–functional analysis. By adopting a different progression system, what must be only a nonfunctional chord with respect to the tonal–functional system can be transformed into a chord with a specific harmonic direction—V/vi becomes a special kind of DP chord in Op. 10/1, if nowhere else. Of course, such systems are only occasionally this useful in straightforwardly tonal pieces, but they are indispensable in dealing with music of the late "recalcitrant" tonal literature (e.g. Mahler, Strauss, early Schoenberg).

Progression systems within the domain of form prolongations are familiar to most musicians. We normally apply formal labels in certain orders, which depend on the larger-level prolongations heard. For example, we label with "A," "B," "A," "C," and "A" in that order if we have applied "(five-part) rondo." We do not usually sort formal things into functional categories.

Progressions of horizontal prolongations are relatively unfamiliar. However, thinking in terms of progressions of motives could produce a sense of directedness and coherence similar to that which we associate with chord progressions as revealed by exceptional analyses. Unlike chord progressions, it is almost inevitable, but not undesirable, that each piece will suggest its own particular system of motivic progressions. Figure 6.10D presents a series of motivic progressions in Brahms's Op.

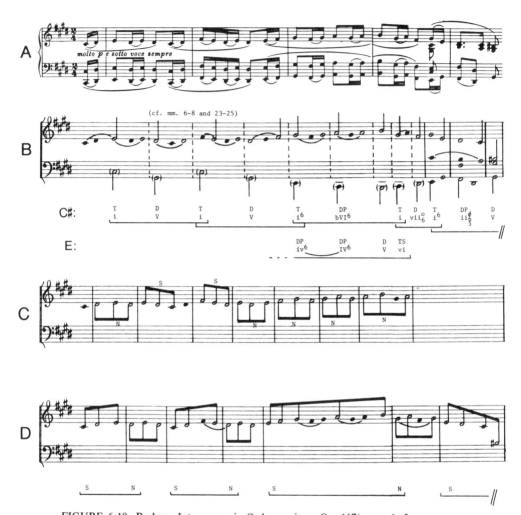

FIGURE 6.10. Brahms, Intermezzo in C-sharp minor, Op. 117/, mm. 1–5.

Vocabulary: (B) diatonic triads and seventh chords from C-sharp (minor) and E (major) (progressions as above)

(C, D) three-event neighbor figures with respect to (C-sharp minor) diatonic universe (functional category N); (C-sharp minor) diatonic scale figures, any length (functional category S)

Progression paradigm: (D) S – N

117/3, based on the vocabulary and paradigm shown; the truncation of these motivic progressions in this first "phrase" correlates with the chordal incompleteness of the truncated progression (half-cadence) shown in Figure 6.10B. As is often the case with motivic progressions, functional categories are specified in the same terms as the prolongational vocabulary. The description of motivic progressions focuses on lines and common pitches; compare the first two progressions in Figure 6.10D, for example. Some of the residue with respect to Figure 6.10D is shown in 6.10C; these are all possible prolongations, none of which figure in the progressions at hand.

Figure 6.11 is a more elaborate example, showing a striking interaction between high- and low-level motivic progressions in the first eight measures of the Goldberg Variations. Here the same motivic progression found $3\frac{1}{2}$ times in the upper voice (Figure 6.11D) also subsumes that entire upper voice (Figure 6.11E). Octave equivalence must be powerfully invoked throughout in order to hear this compatibility. The events incorporated in motivic prolongations are for the most part chord tones in a fairly obvious chord-prolongational characterization of the passage (Figure 6.11B and C).

Interlude: Progressing beyond Tonality

Most of this chapter concerns tonal analysis—what we make of pieces we regard as tonal, even if from a not-very-tonal point of view. However, the same kind of prolongation–progression approach can be applied to pieces in which the traditional chord progressions are difficult to hear persuasively and which we can therefore think of as nontonal. Most of us have weak expectations about the sorts of things we will prolong in what orderings in nontonal pieces approached for the first time; thus nontonal analyses are usually evaluated more in terms of interest than appropriateness. As in motivic analyses, each piece will probably suggest its own individual progression systems, usually based on nontriadic vocabularies.

In working out reasonable prolongations to be heard in nontonal pieces, the distinction between horizontal and vertical is much less relevant than it is with respect to tonal music. Prolongation vocabularies will be specified in terms of intervals or interval classes, with no special connection between "steps" and the horizontal, or between larger intervals and the vertical. Of course, the further notion of diatonic subcollections within the 12-pitch-class universe will be useful only with respect to a few pieces.

The range of progressions that can be concocted is limited only by the extent of our creativity. We find recurrent successions of segments char-

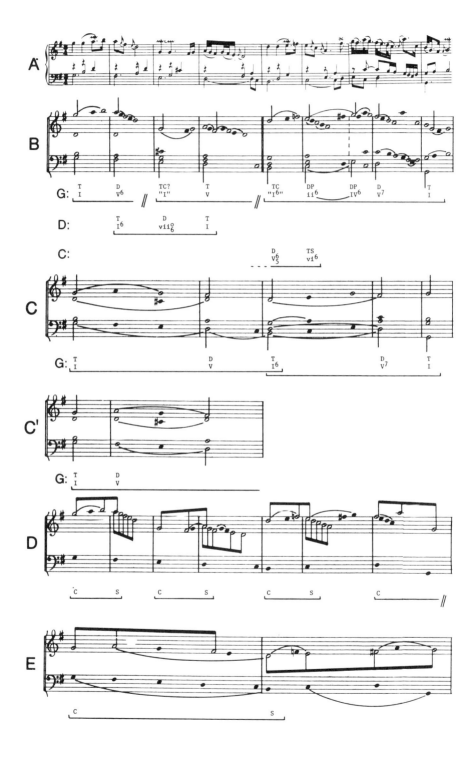

acterized as certain things, and, by predetermining what will count as a progression of these prolongations, transform pieces from directionless successions of events into coherent things. For example, Berg's song, "Schlafend trägt man mich in mein Heimatland," Op. 2/2, can be heard in terms of prolongations of the six possible "French sixth" chords, so that the harmonic language of the entire piece can be heard as deriving from the opening sonorities. It is productive to hear seven-chord progressions, each of which cycles through all six of these chords and returns to its first member.[14] The middle portion of the song manifests these prolongations and progressions less clearly than either the beginning or the end; mm. 9–12 can therefore be characterized as relatively developmental, and the end of the song as a more direct rewrite of the opening.

Figure 6.12 is a sketch of prolongations and progressions that can be heard in Webern's Op. 10/4. Figure 6.12A shows three overlapping prolongations of the 12-pitch-class aggregate. Figure 6.12B shows three two-unit progressions, each a (0–2–6) sonority followed by a three-event sonority containing an interval-class 1. Figure 6.12C shows two complete and one truncated two-unit progressions, each an occurrence of pitch-classes D, Ab, and Eb followed by a (0–1) sonority; it is also possible to hear Figure 6.12C as laying out a single five-unit progression subsuming the entire piece.[15] Figures 6.12B and C are just two of a large number of such progressions that can be devised; eventually, given enough imagination and persistence, every event in Op. 10/4 could be heard to play many different functional roles, in a wide range of progressions. Such a multiple characterization might well reflect that aural opacity many of us hear in early Webern—or at least reflect it more closely than any ascription of just one role in one segmentation to each event.

14. The first progression may be notated, in terms of sets of pitch classes (C = 0): (2, 4, 8, 10)—(1, 3, 7, 9)—(0, 2, 6, 8)—(1, 5, 7, 11)—(0, 4, 6, 10)—(3, 5, 9, 11)—(2, 4, 8, 10).

15. In the fourth segments of both Figures 6.12B and C, there are three separate manifestations of the prolonged sonorities, (0–1–6) and (0–1), respectively. For the purposes of these sketches these transposed sets can be considered multiple appearances of just one thing, much as revoicings of a chord within one chord prolongation can count as "the same thing."

FIGURE 6.11. J.S. Bach, Aria (theme) from the "Goldberg" Variations, mm. 1–8.

Vocabulary: (B, C, C′) diatonic triads and seventh cords from G (major), D (major), and C (major) (progressions as above)

(D,E) three-event cambiata figures, with respect to (G major and C major) diatonic universes, intervals of a third and second, any contour (functional category C);

(G major) diatonic scale figures, any length (functional category S)

Progression paradigm: (F,F) C – S

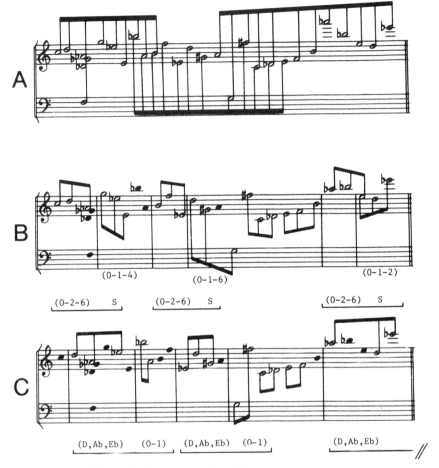

FIGURE 6.12. Webern, Orchestra piece, Op. 10/4.

        Vocabulary: (A) collections of 12 pitch classes (aggregates)

                   (B) (0–2–6) sonorities; three-event sonorities each containing a (0–1) sonority (functional category S)

                   (C) (D, Ab, Eb) sonorities; (0–1) sonorities

     Progression paradigms: (B) (0–2–6) – S

                       (C) (D,Ab,Eb) – (0–1)

Syntaxes—Strategies

> Whenever simplicity and conservatism are known to counsel opposite
> courses, the verdict of conscious methodology is on the side of simplicity.
> Conservatism is nevertheless the preponderant force, but no wonder: it can
> still operate when stamina and imagination fail.
>
> —W. V. Quine, *Word and Object* (Cambridge:
> MIT Press, 1960), pp. 20–21

A prolongation vocabulary and a progression system based on that vocabulary can be jointly referred to as a *syntax* for any piece to which it is
applied.[16] A musical syntax is in this sense something like a systematic
listening strategy.

The term "syntax" is borrowed from both formal logic and linguistics,
but is used here in a specifically musical sense. The syntax of a formal
logic consists of a set of symbols and a set of formation rules determining
which strings of symbols are well-formed "sentences" in that logic; the
twofold structure of vocabulary plus orderings outlined above for musical
syntaxes is inspired by this logical model. However, in order to be useful,
a logical syntax must be decidable; there must be effective procedures for
determining whether any string of symbols is well formed or not. Such
procedures are out of place in musical thought. What possible value could
there be in deciding absolutely whether, say, the third chord in Figure
6.11B is or is not a chromatic tonic substitute, as well as a dominant in the
key of D? The musical point of that chord is that it is and it is not; each
way of hearing the chord leads to a valuable way of hearing the passage.
Is the first progression in Figure 6.11B truncated or not? (It is notated as
truncated; but it is also reasonable to hear a three-chord progression over
mm. 1–3, comprising T–D–T.) Is the sixth segment in Figure 6.11B one
complex dominant preparation chord or two more straightforward
chords? We rarely bother to decide such questions, since access to conceptual richness in music has more to do with the formulation of alternative hearings.

Syntax in linguistics is the level of sentence analysis at which sentences
are represented as certain approved sequences of meaningful units; similarly, a musical syntax is a strategy for hearing pieces as embodying certain orderings of things that might be said to be meaningfully characterized (prolongations). But the point of linguistic analysis is to isolate the
one best syntactical approach for any given group of sentences, a language—a syntax that will completely account for the syntactical aspect of

16. The usage I prefer is to talk of syntaxes' being more or less productively applied to
pieces, rather than to speak of discovering the syntax(es) of a piece.

that language. After an initial period of acclimation, musical thinking is handicapped by a preoccupation with just one syntax for any group of pieces. Some syntaxes, especially the tonal syntax, may seem so successful at characterizing certain pieces that we may be tempted to talk of a "best syntax" now and then; but even the most rampantly productive syntax is never the *only* productive analytical perspective. To avoid the others in the name of treating music as a language is to minimize the music.

It should now be clear why musical functionality is relative. Without specifying a syntax, talk of the function of an event is literally vacuous. *With respect to a syntax,* we can characterize an event's function(s) by citing the roles it plays within the component prolongations of any relevant progressions. Function is not absolutely determined by any such specification; an event may have many distinguishable functions with respect to just one syntax, and often has incomparable functions with respect to different syntaxes. Adopting several different perspectives usually leads to a richer characterization than restricting an analysis to just one syntax.

The value of one-perspective analyses should not be minimized, however. I have already suggest that appropriateness be aligned with the application of musical syntax(es). We say that an analysis of some piece is appropriate if it is based on a syntax we know well in the context of analyses of similar pieces; the more familiar a syntax, the more appropriate that analysis seems. An analysis that makes extensive use of a familiar syntax or that develops its one perspective so extensively as to create its own syntax can be indispensable.

Appropriateness is not an absolute standard. Even given a familiar syntax we agree is applicable to some piece, there will seldom be a single most appropriate analysis of that piece. There may well be alternative progressions, of comparable scope, all of which could be considered appropriate characterizations of some passage, and none of which can be clearly preferred to the others. Successful analyses will probably incorporate some, but not necessarily all, of these alternatives; it is possible, then, that equally appropriate analyses could be virtually incomparable.

Nor is appropriateness an objective matter; it is not a property of an analysis considered apart from the opinions and predispositions of its perpetrator and victims. But neither is it a purely subjective notion. It is possible for me to render my ideas about appropriateness accessible, if not transparent, to others, by delineating the prolongation vocabularies and progression systems that make up the syntaxes I know, and by outlining the syntaxes I hope to develop.

There is a potential for this kind of syntactical working out in all analyses. Translating an analysis into this general form can reveal the extent of systematic assumptions underlying that analysis, and can help the analyst transcend the normative to the individual and contextual—the interesting. For appropriateness is the manifestation of a conservative tendency in analysis, the tendency to utilize the familiar, to characterize things in ways already explored, to gather together pieces into literatures by focusing on their similarities from well-known points of view, to promote the systematic and the more or less deductive modes of musical thought.

Striving after interest, on the other hand, can be seen as a tendency toward novelty, toward hearing things in ways not tried before, toward finding similarities between things that are incomparable according to established strategies, toward experimental and inferential approaches. The beginnings of interest are found in the descriptions of prolongations and progressions, and in the discussion of residues; the end is nowhere in sight. Because our desire for interesting analyses causes us to construct new metrics of similarity and to subsume old differences, I associate interest with an innate drive for simplicity, and with inductive thought in general. Furthermore, although it is easy to characterize systems and deduction by invoking what we call "logic," it is next to impossible to normalize inductive thinking or to isolate the bases for judgments of simplicity and similarity; this difficulty is, of course, inherent in the nature of inductive thought.

Although the relation between appropriateness and interest is dichotomous, it is not static. When we encounter remarkably interesting characterizations, we often extract particular statements and systematize. The analytical life cycle runs from syntactical thinking at first close encounters with pieces, to augmentation of syntactical characterizations with whatever interesting observations suggest themselves, to the development of new syntaxes from the most promising of the novelties. Appropriateness continually yields priority to interest, but it feeds on it as well; the most interesting things we can say at any given time eventually become incorporated into our everyday analytical language, and must then be superseded by further experimentation.

Appropriateness and interest are best thought of not as standards but as directions an analysis can take. Furthermore, instead of being jointly achievable goals, they turn out to be complementary; if directions, they seem to be quite different directions. For an analysis to come across as both appropriate and interesting requires a careful balancing act, of the familiar and the systematic against the novel and the inferential. But it can hardly come as much of a surprise to realize that any endeavor as creative as musical analysis is best pursued by means of a prudent mixture of the logical and the intuitive, the deductive and the inductive, the conservative and the experimental, the cautious and the carefree.[17]

17. This chapter has been incorporated as part of the author's Ph.D. dissertation, "Patterns and Strategies: Four Perspectives of Musical Characterization" (The University of Michigan, 1980).

A

Accent: in poetry, 39

Aesthetics. *See* Esthetics

Adjukiewicz, K.: on categorical grammar, 157n, 159n

Analyses: as appropriate or interesting, 139–42; as perceived by particular musicians, 139; strategies of, 139

Analytic language: development of, 83–84; music as, 100

Appropriateness: of analyses, 139–42; not same as truth, 141; and alternative syntaxes, 172

Austin, Larry: *Continuum* (1964), 44

B

Bach, J. S.: *Sonata for Solo Violin in C minor, Largo,* BWV 1005, 13–20; *"Goldberg" Variations, Aria,* 167–68

Bamberger, Jeanne: metric response to pulses, 101–2

Bassbrechung: as a melodic phenomenon, 31

Basso continuo. See Fundamental bass

Berg, Alban: *"Schlafend trägt man mich in mein Heimatland",* Op. 2, No. 2, 169

Binary processing: explanations for, 102

Block design: defined, 63; in ETS 11, 68. *See also* Cyclic block design

Brahms, Johannes: *Intermezzo in E,* Op. 116, No. 6, 140–42, 145–55, 156–57; *Intermezzo in C-sharp minor,* Op. 117, No. 3, 165–67

C

Cadence: at the pitch-class level, 7; in Rameau's definition, 29–30

Chopin, Frederic: *Etude in C minor,* Op. 25, No. 12, 155–56; *Etude in C,* Op. 10, No. 1, 161–65

Chord progression: vs. lines, 1–2; generated by melodic activity at surface, 28

Chord successions: in tonal pieces, 139; containing embellishing sonorities, 140–41; as a vocabulary of vertical prolongations, 151; non-chord sonorities in, 154; as chord progressions, 158. *See also* Prolongation; Progression

Chromaticism: inflection in pitch-class models of, 8; extent of background inflection of, 27

Coker, Wilson: on pulse, 38n

Communication theory: and rhythmic structure, 55

Counterpoint: of repeating musical units, 40

Cyclic block design: not in ETS 12, 62; generated by difference sets in some ETS, 62; defined, 63; table for ETS 11, 64; table for ETS 13, 65–66; in ETS 13, 67; in ETS 31, 80